TRADE AND POLITICS ON THE COROMANDEL COAST SEVENTEENTH AND EARLY EIGHTEENTH CENTURIES

Trade and Politics on the Coromandel Coast

Seventeenth and Early Eighteenth Centuries

Radhika Seshan

PRIMUS BOOKS

PRIMUS BOOKS
An imprint of Ratna Sagar P. Ltd.
Virat Bhavan
Mukherjee Nagar Commercial Complex
Delhi 110 009

Offices at CHENNAI KOLKATA LUCKNOW
AGRA AHMEDABAD BENGALURU COIMBATORE DEHRADUN GUWAHATI
HYDERABAD JAIPUR KANPUR KOCHI MADURAI MUMBAI PATNA RANCHI

First published 2012

ISBN 978-93-80607-25-2

Published by Primus Books

Laser typeset by Replika Press Pvt Ltd, Kundli, Haryana
Printed at Sanat Printers, Kundli, Haryana

To
My Family

Contents

Acknowledgements

THIS IS A fairly extensively revised version of a doctoral thesis that I submitted many years ago. The thesis itself was long in completion, and the subsequent publication has taken almost as long, if not longer. In the process, of both the thesis and its publication, I have been helped immensely by a great many people. My gratitude goes first to Professor Muzaffar Alam, then in the Centre for Historical Studies (CHS), Jawaharlal Nehru University, New Delhi, for his constant encouragement. Professor R. Champakalakshmi, also of the CHS, went through the early drafts in great detail. The late Dr Sushma Varma, of the University of Pune, was a source of encouragement, whenever I got discouraged (and bored) with the writing of the thesis.

My senior colleague at the Department of History, University of Pune, Professor Rekha Ranade, has read bits and pieces of this work, both earlier, in thesis form, and when I was revising it.

I must, in particular, acknowledge the help of many of my students—some, who just kept asking me when I was ever going to publish, and ended up making me feel guilty enough to actually undertake the work of revision, and Shweta for much more concrete help—by way of making the maps, and generally answering all my desperate yells for help with the computer!

Pune RADHIKA SESHAN

INTRODUCTION

'The Time has Come'

'The time has come,' the Walrus said,
'To talk of many things.
'Of shoes; and ships; and sealing wax;
'Of cabbages and kings.
'And why the sea is boiling hot,
'And whether pigs have wings!'
LEWIS CARROLL
'The Walrus and the Carpenter'

THE MEDIEVAL period of Indian history has been the focus of much research, but paradoxically, also the area in which there is very little work. Scholarship on the administrative systems, land revenue systems, and, of course, on the state in medieval times has been extensive. On the other hand, regional studies are still in their infancy, especially for the Deccan. Maritime history has acquired greater importance, but again, the focus has been on specific areas—Gujarat, the Malabar Coast, or Bengal, to name a few. In addition, the emphasis has been on trade and trade routes, with scant attention devoted to related matters like shipping techniques, navigation methods, or shipbuilding technology. While it is true that sources for such information are rather insufficient, even aspects of trade, banking, currency systems, for which information is available, have not been studied in any great detail.

Any work would have to begin with justifying the choice of subject, and it is probably axiomatic to justify one's choice in terms of insufficient research. In the context of this volume, the fact is that there are many areas of the economic history of India which still deserve a great deal more attention than they have so far received. One such field is the nature of the links between the mercantile and the other worlds, and the changes that took place in these worlds in the course of the medieval period, within the framework of regional history.

Regional history, in a country like India, with its geographical, cultural and linguistic variations, is not just desirable but necessary. To some extent, south India has been luckier than some other parts of the country, given the number of scholars who have worked, and who continue to work on aspects of south Indian history. Sources for such study are vast, ranging as they do from numerous inscriptions, to scores of texts, and sources in non-Indian languages. However, this very wealth also makes the study more difficult, as it then becomes necessary to choose one's area and focus of research. Therefore, as with other aspects of Indian history, there is very often a rather lopsided kind of research, for some areas and aspects tend to get studied much more than others.

There are numerous preconceptions that have assumed the status of statements of fact about India and Indian trade. A common one, which seems to have been laid to rest at last, is that India had almost no trade, because Indians, concerned as they were with matters spiritual/metaphysical/philosophical, were unconcerned with the material world. Sights fixed on the afterlife, they lived out each day in what was (apparently) a fatalistic blur, in which only calendars—and that too, only the natural one—would have had any meaning. With time being meaningless, the concept of time being money was obviously alien.

The next truism contradicts the first considerably, but the paradox in the two parallel statements has been completely overlooked. Thus, the second says that India had numerous merchants and flourishing trade—these two being the most visibly material in the material world—but the merchants were treated as (or treated themselves as) outside the society they lived and traded in. So there was, on the one hand, the life of the merchants, which was one of conspicuous consumption and tremendous wealth, and on the other, the poor peasant, eking out a miserable existence as best as he could, and fatalistically accepting his lot in life. Naturally, never could the twain meet. India being a predominantly agricultural country, and given the size of the peasant population, it was the latter attitude that was much more dominant. How one can, at the same time, be both concerned with the material world, and work very successfully in such a world, but live in a metaphysically-oriented society, has never been adequately explained.

Linked to this is the third truism, and the one with which this book is most concerned. This is the understanding which accepts trade, traders and the economy of trade as being vibrant, but which then says that the merchants isolated themselves from the political world. Essentially, the statement assumes that different professional/social groups in India occupied different spaces, and while these spaces might overlap on occasion, they were generally distinct and separate. Thus, there was the political world concerned with the king(s), ruling class(es), wars, and the collection of revenue. Then there existed the religious world—spiritual, otherworldly and fatalistic. And then there was the mercantile world—busy with the material universe of money, goods, trade and all forms of exchange. That trade and politics were, are, and will be interlinked is a statement so hackneyed as to be virtually a cliché. However, for Indian history, the belief that the two were separate still holds. This separateness was built into, first, the caste structure, which allowed only one section of the community to engage in trade, and second, to the overwhelming importance given to land and land revenue. As the emphasis was on land, priority was naturally given to those who were entitled to a share in the produce. As such the tiller was not really taken into consideration. Merchants may have dealt in the produce, but unlike the elite, they could not claim a share by right of birth or position. So, like the peasant, they too were to be regarded as unimportant. The widely accepted belief has been that trade was never really seen as an additional source of income for the state, far less as an alternative one. Such statements have more often been made with reference to north India, where the abundance of land permitted the state's dependence on land as *the* primary source of revenue to a much greater extent than in the south. Merchants, in this kind of view, are held to have operated, not precisely in a vacuum, but definitely in a separate world—one that encompassed the sea, which was 'neutral domain', and 'not the concern of the state'.[1]

As a natural corollary to such statements, is the understanding that traders had no role to play in politics. They were on the periphery and remained there; and so, there was no need for them to seek representation or be involved in the politics of the court. Therefore, instances of merchant politicians such as Mahmud Gawan and Mir Jumla are held to be the exceptions that prove the rule. The trading activities of the Mughal family fall into the same category, with perhaps the addition that the Mughals had a keen sense of how to increase their personal income! Again, the basis of such statements was the belief that the world of the traders was distinctly different, and meant to remain so, in the pre-modern world. If this hypothesis is accepted, then it leads naturally to an agreement with the idea that capitalism could not emerge in such a world. If mercantilism as ideology and practice were being seen as basic to the emergence of capitalism, then in the absence of the former, the conditions for the latter were non-existent. This, then, would lead to the equally obvious statement that capitalism was impossible in such a world, for the basic preconditions of a society and polity geared towards capitalism, particularly of the mercantile variety, were absent.

A primary reason for such statements still being accepted is the continued hold that colonial constructions have over certain ideas about Indian history/civilization. Such constructions included, of course, those mentioned earlier, of the spiritual/philosophical bent of mind, but linked to this was also the idea of rationality through science. The spirit of scientific enquiry was declared to be missing in India, which was why there was a supposed tendency towards fatalism (which was demonstrably irrational).

More importantly, science was linked to the material world, and lacking science, the material world was necessarily reduced to mere subsistence. In such a world, technology requirements were minimal.

If technological improvement were the key to progress, there could, obviously, be none in civilizations not rooted in science. Thus was put into place the entire formulation of an absence of scientific temper leading to economic stagnation (due to lack of technology) and an unchanging society, incapable of change from within. That these ideas continue to have an influence is actually, in some ways, a tribute to the efficiency of the construction, particularly as most of these theorizations have been questioned by the increasing body of work on Indian history. They are also testament, unfortunately, to the unquestioning acceptance of certain prejudices as confirmed fact. How trade can function in an environment of insecurity is a question that very few have seen fit to raise; as has the issue of separate worlds. Unless one accepts the Oriental Despotism hypothesis, which argued that the political superstructure was effectively divorced from, and became superimposed on, the economy and social base, one cannot accept the idea of a disjuncture or even a gap between politics and society on a larger scale, and politics and trade in this instance. Issues of productivity, whether of trade or artisanal production or peasant production, were of equal importance to both traders and ruling classes, for these were the sources of income. For the state, it may have been termed revenue, and for the merchant, profit—but the bottom line is that it was income. Both groups would undoubtedly have been interested in, at the very least, maintaining the level of income, if not increasing it. The 'political economy of commerce', as Sanjay Subrahmanyam has termed it, is of immense significance in understanding the pre-modern world.

The change, in the form of closer links between trade and politics, came with the Europeans. They did come as traders, but in the Indian context, found it increasingly difficult to function without a political hold. So, as with Britain after the Industrial Revolution, the final form of the trade-politics link emerged, in the shape of a country ruled by a trading company. Such sweeping statements do not adequately examine the question of how much the East India Company itself really profited from its involvement in Indian politics. While individuals per se amassed huge fortunes, their employers, back home in London, were saved from bankruptcy only by the intervention of the English Parliament. In 1751, Thomas Saunders wrote from Fort St. David: 'We must recognize that if Europeans had not intervened in these affairs and had left Indian princes to resolve their own quarrels, that might have been infinitely more beneficial to trade.'[2] The Company was often dragged into local politics by its own officials in their capacity as private traders, and who then used their official position to bolster their stand.

What, then, was the trading world of the south Indian merchant? To what extent did it continue to include the Bay of Bengal littoral, as a whole, in the seventeenth century? What was the hinterland within which they operated? What were the networks—of trade, of connections (trading, political or any other), or society, of general access and accessibility? To whom or what did they have access, or vice versa? What changed in all this, and to what extent, in the course of the seventeenth century? These are among the questions that need to be asked, and which I have attempted to raise in the course of this work.

The eighteenth century has traditionally been seen as the century of changes—in economic terms, in the idea of the decline of prosperity; in political terms, of course, in the decline of the Mughals, the Anglo-French rivalry, and the final success of the British; and in social terms, especially with regard to the Permanent Settlement and its impact. The eighteenth century debate is an ongoing and vibrant one in Indian history. Given such an emphasis, the seventeenth century has been seen either as the classic period of the medieval (in painting, for instance, this century saw the heights of Indian painting styles under Jahangir, and in architecture, this was the century in which the Taj Mahal was built), or as that which laid the ground for the transition into the eighteenth century, or as the century in which the Mughals finally made their presence felt across India. This kind of writing had focussed on the north Indian perspective, but it also becomes necessary to ask what exactly was happening in the south at this time and through this century.

In many ways, it can be argued that for the south, the seventeenth century was actually a period of transition. Politically, this period saw the final elimination of the Vijayanagar Empire and the southward expansion of the Deccani Sultanates, the entry of the Marathas into the far south and the establishment of a separate Maratha state at Thanjavur, and finally the extinction of Golconda and Bijapur and their absorption into the Mughal Empire. In economic terms, this was a period of immense trade and of profits from trade for the peninsula, especially for the Europeans. Within these contexts, an important question that needs to be raised is, how does one reconcile political insecurity and economic vibrancy? Linked to this is the impact of both the political and economic scenarios on society. Woven into this would be the effect of the Europeans.

The medieval period in the south witnessed the dominance of the two most important southern empires, the Chola and the Vijayanagar. The structures of legitimacy that were established or affirmed in their time by the rulers of these two empires is beyond the scope of this work. What needs to be remembered is that many of the institutions that dominated the social, political and economic scenario of the south were established at this time: for example, the emergence of the temple as an important socioeconomic institution is most closely seen in the south in the Chola period. Through much of the medieval period (particularly the Chola), merchant guilds flourished across the region, and even after references to guild-based activities become less numerous, information about trade and associated activities continue to be easily available. The Chola Empire has been the focus of numerous studies. Aspects of their administrative systems, the expansion of their kingdom, the system of land grants and its impact, and, of course, the magnificence of their architecture, have all been studied. Nor has the study of the state been neglected—thanks in large part to Burton Stein's application of the segmentary state model, in opposition to which numerous studies of the state in south Indian history emerged.

Another area of interest has of course been the Vijayanagar Empire. Numerous travellers[3] to the city and empire have reported on the wealth of the Vijayanagar Empire. All of them commented on the gold coins there. Recent researches are focusing on trying to quantify the gold coins on the basis of hoards that have been discovered, but irrespective of the figures that may actually emerge, the wealth of the south can still be taken for granted—at least in the medieval period. The emphasis has generally been on economy, partly because it was during the heyday of this empire that the Portuguese made their first appearance in Asian waters, to establish themselves at Goa, and partly because of the question of the Tungabhadra Doab and the importance of this micro-region to the relations between Vijayanagar and the Deccani Sultanates. The extension of the segmentary model to include Vijayanagar, as well as the earlier categorizations of Vijayanagar being 'the closest to a military state' have ensured considerable interest in state formation for this period as well.

The continuities and the changes from Chola to Vijayanagar times are quite clear, and the continuities are perhaps most visible in the economic sphere. For instance, though the merchant guilds continued, they became less important; the crafts, particularly the textiles, also retained their importance. But by the seventeenth century, the smaller regions within these larger empires also began to assume greater distinction. One such region is the Coromandel Coast.

The Coromandel Coast is a fairly distinct subregion within south India. Its importance from as early as Sangam times is clear, and the connections of Coromandel ports with the ports across the Bay of Bengal were long established. What I am primarily concerned with here, is not just the economy of the region, but the nature of the links between the trading and political worlds, with particular reference to the seventeenth century and the role of the Europeans on the coast in this century. There have, of course, been many works on the arrival of the Europeans and their methods of functioning. The works of K.N. Chaudhuri,[4] Tapan Raychaudhuri,[5] Holden Furber,[6] S. Arasaratnam,[7] N. Steensgard,[8] Sanjay Subrahmanyam[9] and others remain of importance in understanding the nature and directions of Coromandel trade. One hypothesis that deserves a great deal more attention with reference to south India is Andre Gunder Frank's *Re-ORIENT.* If the seventeenth century was the 'Asian century', what was the place of south India and her trade in this century? The role of Coromandel textiles, in particular, in the spice trade of the Asian and world networks has been underlined often enough. At the same time, J.C. van Leur's theory of the 'peddling trade' has also gained both brickbats and bouquets. Which of the two is more applicable? Or was the reality somewhere in between, with, perhaps, a tilt towards one or the other at marginally different times and in different regions? If the former, then who were the merchants or merchant organizations/corporations involved in making this the Asian century? Or were they all concentrated on the west coast of India? There also exist the two slightly older debates, on Immanuel Wallerstein's world systems theory and its relevance or otherwise to India in the pre-capitalist age, and on whether India had the potential to transform into a capitalist economy. Linked to the last would be the entire problem of the nature of mercantile and state activity and the links between the two in pre-eighteenth-century India.

It is perhaps also necessary to identify the contours of the pre-seventeenth century world, so as to trace the developments and changes of the seventeenth century itself. It is in this context that I am concerned with the issue and nature of the linkages between trade, traders, and politics. A basic assumption here is that such linkages did exist, and so, to some extent, Chris Bayly and Sanjay Subrahmanyam's theory of 'portfolio capitalism'[10] has been used. Assuming that there was a relationship, what changed, when and why? Moreover, what role did the Europeans play in fostering this change, or in providing an alternative structure of operations, once change had been set in motion? Bayly's argument about the merchants forming a base for the establishment of the colonial state through their absorption, in an earlier time, into a trade/brokerage relationship has been challenged, but at the same time, there is a certain validity to the idea. Finally, why is it that, on the Coromandel Coast, something like the 'merchant princes'—the Zamorin of Calicut in our period, on the Malabar Coast, or the port of Aceh and its rulers, or Martanda Varma of Travancore in a slightly later period—never emerged? These are some of the issues that I have attempted to address in the course of this work. It must also be stated here that, very often, I have merely raised the questions, and not tried to provide answers to them.

Our first step should perhaps begin by identifying the geographical region known as the 'Coromandel Coast'. The word itself is a corruption of 'Cholamandalam', one of the regions absorbed into the Chola Empire. Technically taken to mean the stretch of the eastern coastline from Point Calimere in the south to Ganjam in the north, it covers almost the entire stretch of the coast of the modern-day states of Tamil Nadu and Andhra Pradesh. Through most of the medieval period, the coast north of Ganjam was named the 'Gingelly Coast', north of which were the Orissa and Bengal coasts. While the nomenclature was different, and there were numerous kingdoms that existed over the region, both simultaneously and consecutively, there was nonetheless an essential economic unity that underlay the political differences. Perhaps the clearest proof of this comes from the so-called country trade of the period—the port-to-port trade, essentially short distance, but fulfilling a vital purpose.

Throughout the period under review, the coast was usually subdivided into the northern and southern parts, with the river Pennar forming a convenient geographical marker that separated the two. The entire coast was dotted with innumerable ports, all part of the interregional country trade, tapping into the same hinterland. Many of these ports were also connected to ports across the Bay of Bengal. An application of the theoretical framework of the port-city model, which studies port-cities within the broad framework of land and water sites and land and water situations, affirms that Coromandel ports were not distinguished by any particularly outstanding geographical feature, either for land or water. 'Site' in the model refers to geographical and environmental factors, and no port was particularly favoured over any other in such factors. 'Situation', which is concerned with extra-economic factors, was far more important—this actually led to the greater dominance of any one port over the others. As it was the politics of the interior and the hinterland of the port that finally helped the development of the port, it is hardly surprising that most Coromandel ports had what S. Arasaratnam has called the 'prosperity-decline' curve.

Moving southwards along the coast, the first port of significance was Bimlipattinam. Mainly involved in the country trade, i.e. port-to-port trade along the coast, by sea, and specifically in the movement of rice up to Bengal and down to Sri Lanka, it began to be more important to the Europeans, especially the Dutch, because it was the centre of a fairly large textile-producing region. South of Bimlipattinam there was a cluster of ports around the Godavari delta, of which Narsapurpeta was the most important (see Map 1: Ports of Coromandel). The centre of the coast's shipbuilding industry, it was reported that the king of Golconda's ships were built here.[11] The dockyard was able to handle ships of very large tonnage, used both for country trade and in the long distance trade across the Bay. Near Narsapurpeta was Madapollam, a textile-producing centre, known for a special variety of cloth described in the records as 'chequered somewhat fine'.[12]

South of these came Masulipattinam, the major port of the Golconda Sultanate, and the most important one on the east coast for most of the seventeenth century. Perhaps more than any other on the coast, it exemplified

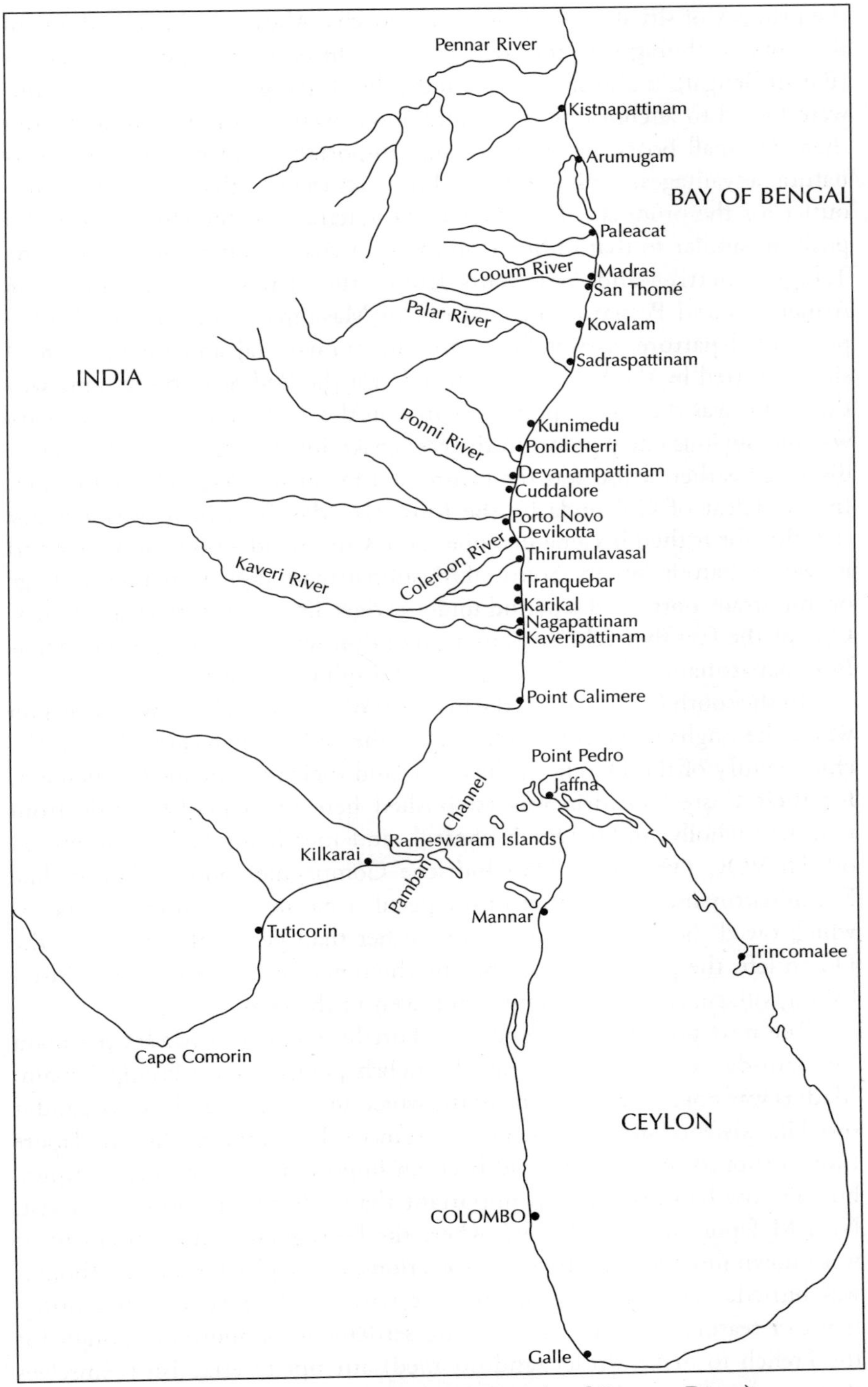

MAP 1: Ports of Coromandel (South of Pennar River)

the primacy of situation over site in a port city. Masulipattinam had one of the worst anchorages on the coast for, in addition to being open to the sea (Bay of Bengal), it also suffered from the disadvantages of a river port. Ships were forced to anchor out at sea, and goods were transported to and from them in small boats. Masulipattinam's importance did not stem from its natural advantages, for it had none, but from the fact that it was the major outlet for the products of the Golconda Sultanate. It therefore occupied a position similar to that of Surat on the west coast. Indian merchants—the Telugu Chettis—and merchants from other parts of Asia, including Armenians and Persians, operated out of Masulipattinam. It was also the point of departure, as was Surat, for the annual Haj and for the annual ship outfitted by the Sultan of Golconda for the Red Sea. In the same way that Surat was the logical point of entry on the west coast, Masulipattinam was the obvious entry point on the east coast, for in addition to the factors discussed earlier, it too was the centre of a major textile-producing region. In the defeat of Golconda by the Mughals, Masulipattinam was a major casualty, for it then became just one more Coromandel port, no better and no worse than the others. South of Masulipattinam there were no very large or important ports in the period under review, i.e. the seventeenth century. One of the few that achieved any recognition was Petapoli, also known as Nizamapattinam, where the English had a minor factory.

In the south Coromandel, the first port of any importance was Armagon where the English established a factory in the 1620s. Then came Pulicat, the chief factory of the Dutch on the coast, and their first fortified settlement, for their Casteel Geldria was established here in 1611–12. Trade from here was wholly under Dutch control, and merchants had to submit to official VOC (Verenigde Oost-Indische Compagnie) policy. Pulicat, like Masulipattinam, is illustrative of the peculiar nature of Coromandel ports, which owed their existence to factors other than geography; for once the Dutch left, the port declined, until by the nineteenth century it was just a fishing village, rendered unimportant even in the coastal trade.

The next port of importance was Fort St. George or Madraspattinam (modern-day Chennai), the seat of English power. Like Masulipattinam, Madras was noted for being one of the worse anchorages on the coast, and it owed its existence and subsequent importance solely to the English. Mylapore (now a suburb of Chennai) had been an important port in ancient times, but by now had become less important than other ports along the coast. Near Mylapore was San Thomé, where the Portuguese had a settlement; it was known more for its religious associations, as the place where St. Thomas was buried, than for its commercial activity. In the seventeenth century, it was a reasonably important trading settlement—important enough for the French to make a brief (and doomed) attempt to establish themselves there.

South of Madras were numerous ancient ports—Sadraspattinam, Pondicherri, Devanamapattinam, Porto Novo (the base of the Indian Muslim merchants known as 'Klings' and 'Chooliars'), Tranquebar (where the Danes had a fort) and Nagapattinam (taken from the Portuguese by the Dutch in the late 1650s). Almost all these ports tapped the weaving villages of the modern-day Nellore, Chingleput, and north and south Arcot districts.

All these ports tapped into the same broad hinterland, covering the modern-day states of Tamil Nadu and Andhra Pradesh. Of course, the existence of traditional trade routes across the subcontinent meant that no region was isolated from any other, and that there was movement of products and produce across India. Therefore, in some ways it could be argued that, allowing for the restrictions of pre-modern transport systems, in general all goods were available across India. That said, naturally there were local specificities and the major product of this region was cotton cloth.

Coromandel cloth had been important in the Asian trade since antiquity. While this was the most important product, and the one most important in the bulk trade, there were also other items, including rice, which were part of the long distance trade, both internal and external. In the seventeenth century in particular, there were diamonds from the Golconda mines. Thus, in this seventeenth-century peninsular region, given the rather low amount of fertile land available for cultivation, and the existence of a vibrant handicraft economy, it is not surprising that the political powers there regarded trade as a major source of income. The actual extent of income derived from taxation of mercantile economy is rather difficult to determine, but the range of support given by the states to merchants and trade is indisputable. The main focus of this work will therefore be to try and understand both, the nature of these links in earlier times, and the changes that occurred as a result of the breakdown of that earlier system during the seventeenth century.

Notes

1. S. Arasaratnam, *Maritime India in the Seventeenth Century,* Delhi: Oxford University Press, 1994, p. 174.
2. Quoted by H. Furber, *Rival Empires of Trade in the Orient 1600–1800*, Minneapolis: University of Minnesota Press, 1976, p. 156.
3. As for an example in the account of Abdur Razzaq or that of Nicolo Conti.
4. K.N. Chaudhuri, *The Trading World of Asia and the English East India Company, 1660–1760*, Cambridge: Cambridge University Press, 1978; K.N. Chaudhuri, *Trade and Civilisation in the Indian Ocean: An Economic History from the Rise of Islam to 1750*, Cambridge: Cambridge University Press, 1985.

5. Tapan Raychaudhuri, *Jan Company in Coromandel Coast, 1605–1690: A Study in the Interrelations of European Commerce and Traditional Economics*, The Hague, 1962.
6. H. Furber, *Rival Empires of Trade in the Orient*, op. cit.
7. S. Arasaratnam, *Merchants, Companies and Commerce on the Coromandel Coast, 1650–1750*, Delhi: Oxford University Press, 1986.
8. N. Steensgard, *The Asian Trade Revolution of the 17th Century: The East India Companies and the Decline of the Caravan Trade*, Chicago: University of Chicago Press, 1974.
9. Sanjay Subrahmanyam, *The Political Economy of Commerce: Southern India 1500–1650*, Cambridge: Cambridge University Press, 1989.
10. Sanjay Subrahmanyam and Chris Bayly, 'Portfolio capitalists and the political economy of early modern India', in *Merchants, Markets and the State in Early Modern India*, ed. Sanjay Subrahmanyam, Delhi: Oxford University Press, 1990, pp. 242–65.
11. R.C. Temple, ed., Thomas Bowrey's *A Geographical Account of the Countries Around the Bay of Bengal, 1669–1679*, London: Hakluyt Society, 1905.
12. H.K. Sherwani and P.M. Joshi, eds., *History of Modern Deccan, 1295–1724*, 2 vols., Hyderabad: Government of Andhra Pradesh, 1973, p. 25.

CHAPTER 1

'To Talk of Many Things': The Trading World of pre-Seventeenth Century Coromandel

THE TRADING world of Asia had had its patterns and networks well established long before the seventeenth century. Driven by the annual monsoon winds, there was a set and traditional operating system, governed by the demand for spices, horses and textiles. The best spices were, of course, to be found in the eponymous 'Spice Islands'—the Indonesian islands. While the spices from these islands were in great demand all over Asia and Europe, the islands themselves did not have a very extensive money economy, and so, the prime unit of exchange for these spices was Indian, particularly Coromandel textiles. India herself throughout the medieval produced most of what she needed and consumed, with the exception of horses. Cavalry was the most important wing of the medieval Indian armies, but the best horses came from Arabia. Thus, the basis for the three-way movement of goods, with Indian textiles being an important pivot, came to be established very early in Asian trading history.

Geographically, too, India was the pivot. The Indian Ocean network had Africa on one side, and South-East Asia and China on the other. India was obviously central in this sense as well, for in the age of sail, when travel was entirely dependent on prevailing winds and currents, it would probably have been impossible to bypass India altogether even if the desire to do so were present. Culturally and politically, too, India was welcoming, for not only were all the religions then dominating the Asian world also practiced here, but over the centuries, kinship ties had been established across Asia—for example the Turkish family of the Chellaby's, who operated through their family ties in Turkey, Persia, and the Red Sea area, in addition to Gujarat and the Mughal Empire later.

When, as mentioned earlier, India was both a large-scale consumer of an expensive item and a producer of a range of products (the latter being more important in the period under review), it is hardly surprising that the Asian trading world came to be essentially centred on India. The country apparently had an unending capacity to absorb gold and silver, but did provide goods that were worth their value in these metals, prime among which was cloth. The textile industry of pre-modern India was an extremely well-organized, compartmentalized and efficient one, in which production could expand to meet new demands, as happened in the seventeenth century, with the increased European demand.

Given the modern acceptance of and dependence on factory production, it is easy to forget that under the rubric of 'textile industry' were subsumed a great many industries. Today, the silks of south India are world-famous, but during the seventeenth century, the Coromandel was renowned mainly for cotton cloth. Quite apart from the production of the raw material—cotton in this case—there were included numerous specific operations, including spinning of the yarn, weaving, bleaching, dyeing and painting or printing. Each was actually an industry in itself, again with its own internal specializations and traditions. Some families may have been involved in the entire process, but in such cases the quantity produced was probably not very large, i.e. for domestic consumption only. Weavers may have been the most numerous, but the very fact that there were distinct activities, with members of each craft carrying a specific caste identity, points both to the number and to their visibility in society and economy.

Weaving was obviously a very important profession, and weavers in earlier times apparently enjoyed many privileges. The Madras Museum Copper Plates of Uttama Chola provide glimpses of such privileges, which could include temple management and the maintenance of temple accounts. Interest on paddy and money accruing on investments by the temple was to be apportioned among the different shrines, and two weavers were entrusted with this task.[1] Whether such privileges continued into the seventeenth century is unclear, but it is likely that they did, for hints of their traditional privileges are to be found in accounts of the clashes between the left hand and right hand (*idangai-valangai*) castes.

Mention is made of many weaver communities, of which the most important in earlier times were the Devanga, Saliya and Kaikkolar. The last were believed to combine military activities with weaving during the Chola period, but became full-fledged weavers with the establishment of the Vijayanagar Empire. They usually settled in the streets around a temple (as can be made out, even today, by a purely cursory look at the street names in the major textile towns of the south, like Kanchipuram and Madurai). A tax was levied on each loom, with concessions being made if a single family owned a large number of looms.[2] Other inscriptions mentioned, for instance a tax of two *panam* on the loom of each Kaikkolar weaver living near a particular temple.[3] Early in the seventeenth century, an inscription from the south Arcot district records an agreement by the weavers to pay a small sum every month, 'for the encouragement given to them to resettle in the village, . . . when owing to hard times they had emigrated to other places'.[4] Later in the same century, however, besides the Kaikkolar, who are called 'trouble makers',[5] the only other weaving caste specifically mentioned is that of the 'Janrawar', who were persuaded to settle in the vicinity of Fort St. George.[6]

The skills of the weavers are well attested to by the Europeans. Patterns were dictated by tradition; and the Europeans, to their disgust, found that minor variations in design, of no significance to the weavers themselves, could result in the entire stock becoming unacceptable in a particular region. The degree of specialization is well brought out as early as 1538, in an inscription which goes into the details of how much yarn is to be used in a particular kind of look, in what fashion, and by whom.[7] This, however, did not in any way mean that the weavers were incapable of innovation, for in 1696, the factors reported that all the looms in Udayar Palayam had been altered to meet the English East India Company's requirements.[8] Newer patterns, to suit European tastes, were given to the weavers, who were able to follow them easily enough. One of the rare complaints from the artisans in the English records comes from 1696, when the painters said that they 'did not understand Painting with a good Chay [a root used for a red colour]', as they had always worked on coarse cloth, 'with a more ordinary Chay'. However, one person from among the painters later volunteered to teach the others, as he understood the new method.[9] Some attempt was made to get weavers in the south to make cloth 'after the Bengal fashion', but this was apparently unsuccessful. It appears that some individuals had also emerged as 'master weavers',[10] while other weavers had taken to selling the cloth they made. References to 'Cilai Cettis' are found fairly early;[11] and in 1694, the factors complained that two 'merchant weavers' had forced the weavers to make the 'Manilha sort of cloth' instead of that required by the Company.[12] Shortly afterwards, the Company entered into contracts with these merchants for the supply of the Company's cloth.

While we do not have names of very many different varieties of cloth prior to the sixteenth century, thereafter, we do have the names of numerous cloth varieties. However, Coromandel cloth was classified as painted ('pintadoes'), or printed. In the former, as the name indicates, the design was painted on to the cloth, in accordance with a pattern (usually a traditional one), while in the latter, designs were printed with a block (often wooden) on which the design had been engraved. In the late nineteenth century, it was stated that Indian cotton fabrics were of three kinds: (i) block-printed only; (ii) block-printed and handpainted; and (iii) handpainted only.[13] Different areas produced various kinds of cloth. So, the best 'paintings' came from the area around Masulipattinam, while the south Coromandel produced good printed calicos. However, there was no hard and fast rule, and in fact, perhaps the only typical cloth of the Coromandel was the longcloth, so named because of its unusual length.[14] Outside Persia, the best Persian-style carpets were produced near Elluru, in the Golconda kingdom,[15] but as mentioned earlier, Coromandel was known primarily for its cotton textiles.

Dyeing with vegetable dyes was well known, with primary colours like red being particularly famous.[16] As a major element of the dyeing process was the washing of the cloth, settlements of what the Europeans termed 'washers' were found dotted along all the major rivers, in particular along the Godavari.[17] Late in the eighteenth century, there was immense curiosity about the methods used in making dyes, for Indian dyes were reported to retain their brightness for far longer than those used in England, quite apart from the range of colours that were to be found. Turmeric, the root of the madder plant, and mustard, used in association with certain minerals, seem to have played a vital role in making dyes. Once washed and dyed, the cloth had to have designs, which could be painted or printed. For printing, a block with a design engraved in it was used—which implied that the printers had some connection with carpenters. There would have been a well-established network of such linkages between the various artisan groups, but these relationships still need to be studied, and have not been discussed here.

If cloth production was one side of the picture, trade was the other. Numerous scholars have highlighted the position of trade in the south Indian economy. It was, in fact, crucial to the early urbanization of south Indian, when ports flourished, but where there are no indications of other urban settlements or even of a state structure to be found. The late Sangam epics go into paeans of praise about the way ships looked at sea and in harbour, and can almost be called verbose about the number and variety of goods coming in and going out of the ports. The links—of trade and kinship—that connected the Coromandel Coast with countries on the other side of the Bay of Bengal were well established, if not in the Sangam period itself then definitely long before our period.

As late as the census of 1871, it was reported that 'all castes and classes of people are traders', but the 'chief trading caste is the Chetty, of whose males 42% are engaged in trade. . .'.[18] In our period, we find references to Komatis, Beri Chettis and Balija Chettis (all Telugu Chettis). Tamil Chettis and Brahmans were also engaged in trade. Greater numbers of Muslim traders were to be found in Porto Novo and Nagur rather than in Madras and Pulicat, while members of the Golconda nobility were actively engaged in trade from Masulipattinam. Fryer reported that the Masulipattinam traders were 'well skill'd, and [could] arithmetize the nicest Fractions without the help of Pen and Ink; much given to Traffickle and intelligent in the way of Merchandize. . .'.[19]

Trade here, as elsewhere, can be broadly divided into local, intra-regional and inter-regional, with the last covering both, the other regions within

India, and the broader Indian Ocean network. Major and minor trade routes criss-crossed the peninsula, as is clear from the accounts of Tavernier and Master. Traditionally, Coromandel merchants had been involved in the trade to South-East Asia, though a few ships sailed every year to the Red Sea also. The main areas to which ships from the Coromandel sailed were Tenasserim, Siam, Malaysia, Java, Sumatra and Borneo.[20] Imports included gold from Aden and China, silver from China and Japan, elephants from Ceylon and Pegu, horses from Arabia and spices from Sumatra. Exports mainly consisted of different kinds of cloth, and rice to Aden, Ormuz, and Sri Lanka.[21] Cloth formed the major item.

Merchant guilds handled much of this trade between the eighth and the sixteenth centuries.[22] Inscriptions refer to a great many groups of merchants, such as the Ainnurruvar, Valanjiyar, Nanadesi, Manigramam, Anjuvannam, etc.; the first named, the Ainnurruvar, figure prominently in many inscriptions. The Ainnurruvar (or 500) was a group of itinerant merchants, travelling all over the south. The organization was established in the eighth century at Aihole, most likely as the result of the decision of a group of Mahajans or Brahmans (also called the 500 Swamis of the Mahagrahara of Aihole) to set up an institutional base for the commerce of the region.[23] It has also been suggested[24] that such merchant organizations grew out of small groups of merchants who traded with isolated communities, and who came together for mutual protection. The term '500' retained its conventional usage even after the organization grew in size and composition, comprising people of different castes, religions and regions.[25] As the largest merchant organization, they were said to have mercenaries to protect their goods. They also set up protected mercantile towns called *erivirapattinas*. At the height of their activities, from the eighth century till about the thirteenth century, their reach extended as far north as Kolhapur and Miraj in present-day Maharashtra. Together with other groups, they claimed as their sphere of operations the '18 *pattinams* [possibly ports] . . ., the 32 *velarpuram* [possibly coastal towns involved more in the country trade] and the 64 *kadigai tāvalam* [periodic fairs]'.[26]

The activities of the 500[27] were closely linked to the Cholas, in that they were actively encouraged by the Cholas.[28] The merchants stepped into all the regions that the Cholas conquered, as, for example, the Kongu and Ganga countries after these areas were conquered by Rajaraja I and Rajendra I. In the eleventh century, Aiyapolil Kattur[29] and Basinikonda[30] were made *erivirapattinas* under special charters from the Chola rulers of the region. The former inscription (for Aiyapolil Kattur) calls the 500 the 'virtuous protectors of the Vira Valanjika', consisting of various subdivisions coming from the 'four quarters, the 18 towns, the 32 *velarpuram*, and the 64 *ghatikasthanas*'. It then went on to say that the inhabitants of the new *erivirapattina* were to be exempted from all communal contributions, and that the town was not to be inhabited by those merchants who 'demanded taxes or tolls by threatening people with drawn swords or by capturing them', as well as by those who 'wantonly deprived people of their food or otherwise afflicted them'.[31] Such instances reveal the involvement of merchant organizations in local administration, which apparently took place through the *nagaram*. Hall has identified *nagarams* as marketing centres of a region, as well as 'one among the several indigenous administrative institutions. . .'.[32] The *nagarams* worked in close cooperation with the *ur* or *sabha*. It has been suggested that the *nagaram* was also an assembly, and in those towns inhabited only (or mainly) by merchants, it was probably the only assembly.[33] In Pallava inscriptions, four *nagarams* can be identified[34]—a number that increased considerably under the Cholas, so that there was generally one *nagaram* in each *nadu*.[35] The *nagaram* later became part of the supra-regional trade and so it 'represented the point of intersection between the nadu territory and the wider world of commerce'.[36] It was in this context that the itinerant merchant corporations entered the local field.

The Middle Chola Period (985–1150) experienced a phenomenal increase in the number of *nagarams*, which now came into existence in both the newly conquered areas and in neighbouring kingdoms. They began to be used as 'interdependent agents of political synthesis under the Colas', and so, the *nagarams* became 'part of a wider network of inter-regional and overseas trade'.[37]

The activities of the 500 continued to increase between the twelfth and the fourteenth centuries. At about the same time, weavers also began to organize themselves into guilds. The Kaikkola guild of weavers was supposed to have been divided into four *tisai nadus*, 18 *kilai nadus*, and 72 *nadus*.[38] Kanchipuram began to emerge as the headquarters of the weavers' organizations, and is referred to in numerous inscriptions as *mahanadu*.[39] The guild was expected to handle the affairs of its members, and therefore also dispensed justice when necessary.[40] Various weaver guilds increasingly begin to figure in inscriptions as making donations of different kinds to temples, just as the 500 did. From about the twelfth century, weavers are also mentioned in connection with donations of land.[41]

From the late thirteenth century, craft groups and merchant organizations began to come closer together, and weavers apparently took to trading in textiles. References to Cilai Chettis,[42] merchants trading in cloth, had begun earlier; from the fourteenth century, one comes across weavers who are given the suffix 'Chetti', indicating that they were involved in trade. Weavers-cum-traders formed themselves into the *Saliya Nagarattar*,[43] following which are more references to taxes on looms,[44] and of concessions to weavers to encourage them to settle in certain areas.[45] A fifteenth-century inscription refers to *Narpattenayira* Solakumaran, indicating that he was a master weaver, who employed several weavers,[46] and also that he was by no means exceptional. Other inscriptions of the sixteenth century refer to the Kaikkolas as merchants,[47] as well as master weavers. Inscriptional evidence also points to merchants being involved in gifts of tolls to temples.[48]

Such evidence is indicative of the growing importance of trade, as well as the increased involvement of weavers in trade. This, then, would imply closer connections not just between craft and mercantile organizations, but also between such organizations and local administrative bodies. There was apparently less reliance or royal support, and more involvement at local levels with other organizational groups like the Citrameli Periyanadu or the *Padinen Visaya*. The former was an organization of agriculturists, which has been described as a *periyanadu* (large *nadu*) assembly created by 'the cultivators themselves in order to defend their interests against the centralizing activities of the Cola monarchs'.[49] Such larger *nadus* were, therefore, a 'defensive response by the cultivators, created to protect the vested interests of the local landholding elite (*nattar*) who transferred their political dominance to the new periyanadu assemblies'.[50] The 500 joined such organizations to levy *maganmai* and *pattanapagudi* (tolls and shares of towns). It appears that such levies could be made only in conjunction with such bodies.[51]

Thus, by the fourteenth century, trade organizations were deeply entrenched into local institutions, and came to be intrinsic to the economy of south India. Far from being 'outside' the state, they were an essential part of the local and supra-local agencies of the state, not to be ignored by any king. The extent and degree of change brought about under Vijayanagar rule is still unclear. That trade did not decline is clear from accounts such as that of Abdur Razzaq and the Russian traveller Nikitin, as well as from inscriptions. Weavers and weaving organizations were now more important, and by the twelfth century the Kaikkolas were beginning to claim a higher social status, and granting jewels, etc., to temples in their own right.[52]

Simultaneously, neither were the kings backward in recognizing the importance of trade. It has been suggested that the external policy of the Cholas was considerably influenced by mercantile interests, so that their wars in south Karnataka can be read as an attempt to establish control over the main trade routes between Karnataka and Tamil Nadu, while the attacks on Sri Lanka and Srivijaya, far from being mere plundering raids, can perhaps be viewed as commercial ventures, designed to encourage trade with those areas where pockets of Tamil merchants already existed.[53] The Motupalli grant of the Kakatiya king Ganapati of the thirteenth century, which remitted a large number of taxes on the goods of merchants who traded from and to Motupalli,[54] can be seen in the same light. Approximately one century later, the grant was renewed by Annapota Reddi, who permitted 'the merchants of Motupalli who traded with distant islands and coast towns to stop at their will in their homes at Motupalli and to leave them for other places', without any official pressure. Further, duties on gold and silver were abolished, and merchants were allowed 'the liberty to sell their goods brought from other shores to anybody under any conditions and to carry in exchange, likewise, to other countries any goods they chose'. In addition, it was proclaimed that no cloth was to be detained in the warehouses, and tools on other articles were to be the same as earlier.[55] Furthermore, nayaks or kings were expected to make good the losses suffered by merchants in their areas.[56]

From the fifteenth century, the number of inscriptions referring to merchant organizations begins to decline, and there are only two of any importance in the seventeenth century. One of these, from Narayanavanam (approximately 1620), records the gift of tolls on various articles of merchandise such as cloth, pepper and jaggery.[57] Another, from Lepakshi, mentions Madanna and Akkanna, Golconda's ministers, as the 'best of Brahmins', and states that the 'lords of the Ayyavole both Paradesa and svadesa' led by their chief Prithvi-setti Rayana Bhaskaranna, in consultation with the local caste-guilds, including the tantuvayins [weavers], vastra-bhedakas [cloth dyers] and vastra rakshaka [possibly tailors] fixed certain rates on pack bullocks, looms, etc., as maganmai'.[58] The inscription assumes significance for being one of the rare instances in which a specific merchant is mentioned in connection with the guilds, and because it comes in the seventeenth century, when there are more references to individual merchants than in earlier centuries.

Thus the trading world of pre-seventeenth century Coromandel was not restricted to the Coromandel alone, but spanned the supposedly separate worlds of polity and economy. Trading patterns as established prior to the seventeenth century show that the merchants operated within the existing political framework, and in fact, supported its functioning in numerous ways.

Given the importance of the temple as an economic institution, a related question would be the nature of the links between religion and trade, and the extent to which the temples were bankers, consumers and providers of legitimacy. Perhaps it is in this connection that one needs to interpret the increasing number of inscriptions referring to grants of *maganmai* to temples, or of deposits in temples to be used for specific purposes (providing oil for the lamps, for example). As mentioned earlier, weavers were also accommodated in streets around the temples, as can be seen in the temple town of Kanchipuram even today.

As traders, they had, of course, access to all the production and production areas; and in the same capacity, became crucial to the income of the state. The number of references that we find in the inscriptions to *maganmai* and *pattanapagudi* are testimony enough to the income that could be derived from trade, even without the kinds of connections drawn earlier, between the guild-based activities and the Chola state. Were traders then the bridge between the rural and the urban worlds? If so, their role in linking agrarian and craft production would obviously give them greater importance in both social and political terms. A question that needs to be asked is what changed, and when? Did the links between the polity and the trading world themselves change, or did the method change? Did these links, in other words, become more individual, and less institutional?

Next, where were the Muslim traders in these networks? The European records also refer to activities of the Indian Muslim merchants, called 'Klings' and 'Chooliars'. In the fifteenth and sixteenth centuries, they were referred to as wealthy merchant communities, but early in the seventeenth century, Floris talked of them in the context of the peddling trade, for he said that they brought 'a corge or less of diverse sorts, running with this through all the country, giving the goods so cheap that it is to be admired at . . .'.[59] At the other end of the scale are the references to 'chooliar merchants'[60] who were often wealthy shipowners. In later censuses, four subdivisions were identified among the Chulias—Marakkayar, Labbai, Rawther and Kayalar.[61] The first among these was the wealthiest, and were concentrated mainly in Porto Novo and Nagur. They tended to keep their distance from the Europeans, but had considerable influence at local courts, especially at the court of the Thevar of Ramnad.[62]

While the Europeans were new entrants into this world, it can in no sense be argued that they were the first 'foreigners' on the Indian scene. The Chinese may not have been very familiar faces in the ports, but till as late as the early decades of the fifteenth century, there were Chinese travellers to (particularly) the Malabar Coast, as is testified to by the account of Mahuan. Armenians were a common sight, as were Jews, and both these groups had their own networks that stretched across Southern Europe, North Africa and India, before going on to China.

The pattern of trade that had been established prior to the seventeenth century therefore saw the traders being extremely active both within and without the country. Working within the guilds, they supported, and drew support from, the political system that existed from the Chola period onwards, As has been discussed earlier, they were part of the *nagaram* economy, and their activities were instrumental in linking *nagaram*, *nadu* and the wider world of commerce. The establishment of the Vijayanagar Empire almost certainly brought about a change, visible in the decreasing number of inscriptions referring to the guilds. The question of whether the Vijayanagar Empire was the 'nearest thing to a war state'[63] or not is outside the scope of this research; but it is possible that the armed merchant guilds were considered a threat to the state, and also that protection to the traders was taken over by the nayaks and others, instead. If this is what occurred,[64] then the result would be, first, the deepening of the local base of the merchants, making them much more prominent figures in community life;[65] second, the greater involvement of merchants in politics, and third, the emergence of individual traders rather than trade organizations. The process by which merchants were absorbed into the political life of the state has been pointed out earlier (an increasing involvement in the *nagarams*, or even the instances of granting tolls to the temples). Following this, would be the emergence of important individual traders, as took place in the next century. The seventeenth century was the period of individual traders like Malaya Chetti or Kasi Viranna; of merchants in politics, like Malaya Chetti and Mir Jumla; and finally, of merchants and East India Companies, like Kasi Viranna and Ananda Ranga Pillai.

For the seventeenth century, most of our information about merchants comes from the highly organized textile industry. For bulk production, the involvement of merchants was very necessary, because by the seventeenth century, the weavers operated only with advances from the merchant. A seventeenth century observer put this down to the poverty of the weavers, who, 'between their inbred way of feeding Bramenys and the extortions of their Aveldars, live meerly from hand to mouth. . .'.[66] This seems to be in contrast to the conditions prevailing earlier,[67] but it is possible that the views represent the two extremes, for weaving was both a purely domestic occupation as well as one that catered to a larger market. Nevertheless, by the seventeenth century, dependence on the merchants had probably increased. The system of advances has been compared to the putting-out system, but it should be remembered that only money, and almost never raw materials, was advanced. The advances were given to the merchants, to in turn be given to the weavers. In 1675, the English factors reported that 'here as in all other parts of this Coast, an as we understand at Suratt and the Bay also, as well by the Dutch as English and all others, it has been customary and of course to deliver mony forehand to the Merchants for the more timely accomplishing of their investments . . .'.[68] The advances were necessary for the merchants to get the required quantities of cloth, and the factors in India early on declared themselves in favour of working through middlemen, for fear that 'att the yeares end, when wee expected to be invested of our goods, wee should undoubtedlye come shorte of half our quantitye, besides undergoe a hazard of their [the weavers] running away where there were no hope for us to fynd them'.[69]

What changed with the coming of the Europeans was not the world alone, which had perhaps already begun to change, but the ways in which the new entrants dealt with that world, and also tried to change it to suit their needs. The Portuguese system and attempted monopoly were undoubtedly new methods in Asian waters. Along with such methods of trade, they also brought in new technology, in the form of large ocean-going warships. The use of ships as weapons of war, the assertions of sovereignty over the sea, even if this was, at least in the seventeenth century, not matched by equal sovereignty over land, the competition among the different Europeans for greater access to India's produce—these were the new features that the Europeans brought. The seventeenth-century world for the Coromandel merchant thus ushered in innumerable new features, both on land and at sea—and the former was far more decisive in reshaping their world.

As the first European traders on the Asian scene, the Portuguese tried to impose a monopoly on the existing Asian shipping, through a system of strategically located forts (like Ormuz and Malacca), and by a judicious use of passes, called cartazes.[70] The passes, in all likelihood, were in effect only in Asian waters, used as they were for Asian shipping. The system of a pass, in itself, was not really new. Examples exist of passes being issued by the Chinese. These Chinese passes were, however, usually addressed to the land-based authority, and were framed as a request that the bearer of the pass be given all aid in his ventures. There may have been a concealed threat in the request, but the fact is, it probably could not have been effectively implemented outside the China seas. The Portuguese cartaz, on the other hand, was a clear assertion of their control over the sea and sea routes. Technological superiority over Asian shipping enabled the Portuguese to enforce the system, to which they also linked the idea of *cafilas*—caravans of ships, travelling in convoys, perhaps escorted by the Portuguese. All ships had to have passes, and the Portuguese claimed (and often enforced) the right to stop any ship on the high seas and demand that the cartaz be shown. Any ship not in possession of a cartaz was deemed to be involved in illegal transactions, and both ship and cargo could be seized. This system, backed as it was by an equally judicious use of religion, and the establishment of Portuguese centres variously political, mercantile or religious in nature, ranging from Goa, the seat of the Estado da India, to Macao, was reasonably effective for about a century.

The Portuguese were apparently content with controlling the shipping, and their mixture of sword and Bible in establishing their empire was rather different from that of the other Europeans. Illustrative of this is the fact that they had no major stations on the Coromandel Coast; San Thomé, where there was a Portuguese presence, had religious rather than commercial significance, and Nagapattinam, their only station, was a very minor one in the Estado's scheme of affairs. I would like to draw attention to the fact, that there was a considerable difference between official and private presence. The Estado itself may not have officially occupied itself too much with the Coromandel Coast; but as recent researches have shown, Portuguese presence on this coast was both widespread and important. What they did not have in terms of possessions, they seem to have made up for through influence at the local courts, which they used, with a fair amount of initial success, to block the Dutch entry into the Coromandel.[71]

The system of passes marked the first check on shipping in Asian waters. It is a fact that the Asian merchants soon found alternative routes—Aceh instead of Malacca for instance—but the entry of the other Europeans, who also adopted the system of passes, meant that the merchants had to accept the system as a permanent feature of Asian trade. Another sort of change was obviously the expansion in the size of the market for Indian cloth in Europe. In this, the English trade was of particular importance.

Yet another change was the establishment of what came to be called 'factories' along the coast of India. These factories had, of course, nothing to do with modern factories, being merely warehouses for the goods that were collected prior to being shipped to Europe. They were found to be necessary because of time and distance. Ports, particularly on the west coast, were effectively closed to all traffic during the monsoon, and not only were ships forced to take shelter somewhere in India if they missed the winds, but prices of goods also naturally shot up in the gap of time between arrival and departure of ships. It was therefore felt necessary to have people permanently stationed at various points along the Indian coast so as to make purchases in the off season. In the Mughal and Golconda Empires, permission to fortify these factories was never given, and the earliest forts were all in the far south, in the territories formerly under the Vijayanagar Empire.

By the time the Dutch came on the scene in the seventeenth century, Portuguese power had already begun to decline. Not surprisingly, they (the Dutch) attacked the Portuguese monopoly and possessions vigorously, both by armed attacks on Portuguese factories and ships and by a system of treaties with various local princes. These treaties granted the Dutch exclusive rights of purchase of certain specified commodities,[72] at stipulated prices. Incidentally, they also demanded the exclusion of other European and Asian competitors.[73] In contrast to the Portuguese, the Dutch aim was not just control of shipping, but also control of the trade in spices. As a natural corollary to their interest in spices, their main factories in India were on the Coromandel Coast, where, from Pulicat in the first half, and Nagapattinam towards the end of the seventeenth century, they attempted, with a fair degree of success, to monopolize the trade in spices and later, the products of the Ramnad and Sri Lanka coasts. As their main concern was with the Spice Islands, their headquarters in Asia was located not in India but in Batavia.

The English were still later arrivals, and in the early decades of the seventeenth century, had rather precarious toeholds in the Spice Islands. They had a small factory at Amboyna, but were forced to abandon it when all the Englishmen there were killed in a Dutch attack—the 'Amboyna massacre', as it came to be known. They continued to make attempts to settle factories at Sumatra (York Fort), Bencoolen and Priaman (Atchin, Aceh). However, their focus remained India and her textiles. Perhaps because of their early inability to match the Dutch resources, in terms of both money and ships (of war and trade) they began, at the initial stage, to concentrate much more of their attention on India. This meant, on the one hand, greater attention being paid to selling European goods in India, and on the other, in the interests of profitable trade, to developing a demand for Indian goods in Europe. Indian textiles had long been famous. Within the trade networks, the concentration of the Europeans on the Spice Islands did probably lead to an increase in the amount of traditional cloth manufactured, but the heightened interest in textiles also led to the manufacture of cloth solely for the Europeans. Therefore, if one were 'to talk of many things. . .'., the seventeenth century was definitely a boom period for Indian textiles, and Indian artisans in particular were functioning in extremely favourable market conditions, i.e. whatever they wove was bound to find a buyer.

Notes

1. *South Indian Inscriptions* (henceforth *SII*), vol. III, pt. 3, no. 128.
2. *SII*, vol. IX, pt. 2, no. 516, dated approximately 1526, says that if a single family had ten looms, only nine were to be taxed.
3. *Annual Report on South Indian Epigraphy* (henceforth *ARSIE*), 272 of 1912, the temple at Nerumbur.
4. Ibid., 390 of 1925.
5. H.D. Love, ed., *Vestiges of Old Madras*, 3 vols., London, 1913 (henceforth *Vestiges*, followed by vol. no.), vol. II, p. 29.
6. Ibid., vol. I, p. 547.
7. *Tirumalai Tirupati Devasthanam Inscriptions*, vol. IV, no. 112. This kind of weaving was to be done only by Muslims.
8. Records of Fort St. George (henceforth RFSG), *Letters from Fort St. George*, 18 August 1696.
9. RFSG, *Fort St. David Consultations*, 30 January 1696.
10. *ARSIE*, 221 of 1929–30—an individual was given a site on the condition that he pay four *panams* for every loom set up in it.
11. 'Cilai' is still used in parts of Tamil Nadu to mean sari.
12. Records of Fort St. George, *Diary and Consultation Books* (henceforth RFSG, *Diary*), 5 November 1694.
13. E. Thurston, *The Cotton Fabric Industry of the Madras Presidency*, Madras: Madras Government Press, 1897, p. 13.
14. '72 coveds long by 2 coveds broad', according to the records. A coved measured about 18 inches.
15. R.C. Temple, ed., *The Diaries of Streynsham Master, 1675–1680, and Other Contemporary Papers Relating Thereto*, in 2 vols., London, 1911 (henceforth *Streynsham Master*), R.C. Temple, ed., vol. I, account of journey from Masulipattinam and back to Fort St. George.
16. E. Holder, *Monograph on Dyes and Dyeing in the Madras Presidency*, Madras: Madras Record Office, 1896.
17. The mineral content of the waters of these rivers was a crucial element in fixing the colours.

18. *Report on the Census of the Madras Presidency, 1871*, p. 184.
19. W. Crooke, ed., John Fryer's *A New Account of East India and Persia, Being Nine Years' Travel, 1672–1681*, 2 vols., vol. I, London: Hakluyt Society, 1909, p. 90.
20. B.A. Saletore, 'Some Aspects of the Overseas Trade of Vijayanagar from the Accounts of European Travellers', in *B.C. Law Commemoration Volume*, ed. D.R. Bhandarkar, Calcutta, 1945, pp. 114–27.
21. T.V. Mahalingam, *Economic Life in the Vijayanagar Empire*, Madras: University of Madras, 1951, pp. 110, 113.
22. The term 'guild' is not used in the medieval European sense of an organization of professionals, bound by a set of carefully drawn up rules of conduct, and with definite criteria for membership. Rather, it is used in the sense of 'association'.
23. M.M. Abraham, 'A Medieval Merchant Guild of South India', *Studies in History*, vol. IV, no. 1, 1982, p. 6; M.M. Abraham, *Two Medieval Merchant Guilds of South India*, New Delhi: Manohar, 1988, chap. II.
24. K.R. Hall, *Trade and Statecraft in the Age of the Colas*, Delhi: Abhinav Publications, 1980, chap. 6.
25. M.M. Abraham, op. cit., chap. III.
26. *SII*, vol. VIII, no. 442.
27. Sometimes referred to as the *Nanadesiya Tisaiayirattu Ainnurruvar:* 'The 500 of the Thousand Directions and Several Countries'.
28. Inscriptions of the Pudukottai region, ninth to eleventh centuries, such as the Munisandai inscription (Pudukottai State Inscriptions, no. 61), testify to this in the early period.
29. *ARSIE*, 256 of 1912.
30. Ibid., 342 of 1912.
31. Ibid., 256 of 1912, pt. II.
32. K.R. Hall, op. cit., p. 51.
33. K.R. Venkatrama Aiyar, 'Medieval Trade, Craft and Merchant Guilds in South India', *Journal of Indian History* (henceforth *JIH*), vol. XXV, pts. 1–3, 1947, pp. 269–80.
34. R. Champakalakshmi, 'Developments Within: Urban Processes in the Early Medieval Period A.D. 600–1300', in *Trade, Ideology and Urbanisation*, New Delhi: Oxford University Press, 1996, p. 213, and table IV, pp. 264–87.
35. According to Hall, each *nadu* served as the local marketing territory for the *nagaram*. K.R. Hall, op. cit., p. 130.
36. Ibid.
37. R. Champakalakshmi, op. cit., p. 216.
38. *ARSIE*, 300 of 1909–10. What precisely is meant by these divisions is unclear, but it is perhaps significant that the term '*nadu*' is used, as in Chola times, this was an administrative division.
39. *ARSIE*, 286 of 1910–11.
40. Vijaya Ramaswamy, *Textiles and Weavers in Medieval South India*, New Delhi: Oxford University Press, 1985, p. 40.

41. Ibid., p. 49 and *passim.*
42. *SII*, vol. VII, no. 553.
43. *ARSIE*, 308 of 1913.
44. Ibid., 300 of 1909.
45. Ibid., 390 of 1925.
46. Ibid., 221 of 1929–30.
47. Ibid., 16 of 1935.
48. See, for example, *ARSIE*, 88 of 1914 (thirteenth century).
49. K.R. Hall, op. cit., p. 203.
50. Ibid., p. 204.
51. R. Champakalakshmi, 'The South Indian Guilds', in *Trade, Ideology and Urbanisation*, op. cit., p. 320.
52. Vijaya Ramaswamy, op. cit.
53. R. Champakalakshmi, 'Developments Within . . .' op. cit., pp. 221–5.
54. *ARSIE*, 600 of 1909, p. II.
55. Ibid., 601 and 602 of 1909, p. II.
56. Ibid., 10 of 1920 (copper plate inscription) relates the troubles undergone by a nayak during the occupation of Karnataka by the Nawab of Golconda; 621 of 1920, of Sriranga's time, mentions the remission of taxes of payable by the weavers and merchants for three years on account of the 'plunder suffered by the people'.
57. *SII*, vol. XVI, no. 315; *ARSIE*, 377 of 1911.
58. *ARSIE*, copper plate 18 of 1917–18 and 581 of 1912. The earlier inscription (377 of 1911) also refers to what appears to be the same person, with the difference that he is there called Rayanamantri Bhaskara.
59. W.H. Moreland, ed., *The Voyage of Peter Floris*, London: Haklyut Society, 1934, p. 70.
60. RFSG, *Letters from Fort St. George*, 20 March 1687.
61. *Report on the Census of the Madras Presidency, 1871*, Tamil Nadu State Archives, Chennai and E. Thurston, *Castes and Tribes of Southern India*, vol. IV, Labbai, vol. V, Marakkayar.
62. S. Arasaratnam, *Maritime India in the Seventeenth Century*, Delhi: Oxford University Press, 1994, p. 219.
63. K.A.N. Sastri, *History of South India*, 3rd edn, Madras: Oxford University Press, 1966.
64. This is merely a hypothesis, currently unsupported by any research.
65. In this connection, it is interesting to note that the Nattukottai Chettiars claim to be descended from the Ainnurruvar.
66. W. Foster, ed., *The English Factories in India* (henceforth *EFI*), Oxford: Clarendon Press, 1906–27, n.s., ed. C. Fawcett, 4 vols, vol. II, *The East Coast and Bengal*, pp. 160–1.
67. As mentioned in inscriptions, as also references to 'master weavers'.
68. RFSG, *Diary*, 28 September 1675.
69. *EFI*, 1622–3, letter from Pulicat to the President, p. 104.
70. M.N. Pearson, *Merchants and Rulers in Gujarat*, Berkeley: University of Minnesota Press, 1976.

71. For example, they successfully blocked the Dutch efforts to get a concession to build a factory at Cuddalore, by using their influence at the Vijayanagar court.
72. Something the English objected to later. See E.B. Sainsbury, ed., *A Calendar of the Court Minutes, etc. of the East India Company*, Oxford: Clarendon Press, 1935, the debate regarding the provisions of the Treaty Marine, vol. XXVIII, *passim*.
73. Dutch records, Dutch treaties, 1643–1711; also S. Arasaratnam, 'Mare Clausum: the Dutch and Regional Trade in the Indian Ocean', *Journal of Indian History*, vol. LXI, pts. 1–3, 1983, p. 73.

CHAPTER 2

'Of Cabbages and Kings': Merchants, Trade and Politics

THE EXPONENTIAL increase in demand for Indian textiles by Europeans arose, as is well known, out of the demand for pepper in particular and spices in general. The loss of Constantinople had the immediate effect of closing the land route through which pepper came into Europe, but added yet another reason to search for the sea route to India. The benefits of such a sea route remained obvious even when trade resumed through the Ottoman Empire, for between distrust of the Turks, and the fact of rather more efficient collection of customs duties on goods passing through the Empire, an alternative became imperative. There is no need, here, to repeat the details about the Portuguese success in finding the route, nor in exploring their success in getting control of Goa and establishing the Estado da India. What is far more important is that they immediately set up a supply chain of pepper to Europe, and made an immense profit doing so.

The discovery of the sea route meant the elimination of a great many middlemen. So far, the established patterns had seen Arab or other West Asian merchants, or Chettis, taking Indian textiles to Indonesia, and exchanging them for spices. These spices would then be shipped across to the Persian Gulf or to the Red Sea ports, from where they would be taken overland to the Mediterranean region. At one of these ports—Cairo in particular—groups of Venetian and Genoese merchants would purchase the pepper and take it across into Europe. There were thus at least four groups of merchants of different countries involved in the pepper trade. The coming of the Portuguese and more direct sea routes meant that all these groups were rendered superfluous, for the Portuguese could transport the pepper directly to Europe. To what extent prices actually fell because of this is difficult to determine, as overheads—of transport, profit, or just potential dangers at sea—were possibly higher than before, since they were now handled by just one group rather than so many. But despite this, it is clear that the Portuguese made huge profits, and the quantities of pepper now made available in Europe increased immensely.

It has been estimated that, between 1513 and 1610, each Portuguese ship carried home between 4,345 and 7,891 quintals—approximately 25,000 quintals per year.[1] As mentioned earlier, the Europeans arrived to find a well established trading system, in which Coromandel textiles played a very important role—so much so that, in 1612, the Coromandel Coast was described as the 'left arm of the Moluccas'. Without its textiles, the 'trade in the Moluccas [would] be dead'.[2] This was also a world in which there was virtually no demand for European products, and not very much for bullion.

If, on the one hand, the seventeenth century saw the tremendous opening up of the market for Indian goods, thanks to the entry of the East Indian Companies, it also witnessed both, increased political turbulence in the country, and problems caused due to competition among the various companies. By the 1640s, most of the Coromandel Coast lay within the Golconda kingdom, the richest of the southern kingdoms in the seventeenth century. For instance, as late as 1687, when Golconda had been affected by warfare and the Mughal siege for over a year, it was reported that the treasury contained, in addition to a variety of precious stones and bullion, coined money to the tune of some 7 million gold *hun* and about 20 million silver rupees.[3] The same chronicler further reported that, when the contents of the treasury were finally dispatched northwards, the train of carts (carrying the treasure) stretched for miles.

The century began with warfare in the south. Historically, there had always been trouble between the Sultanates of Golconda and Bijapur and Vijayanagar, and 1565, the Battle of Talikota (Rakshas-Tangadi) has traditionally been accepted as the date of the fall of the Vijayanagar Empire. However, the empire continued to exist, even if it was considerably weakened. Subject to both internal trouble and external threat, the last emperors tried their best to keep things going, without much success. Eventually, civil war broke out in the much truncated Vijayanagar Empire in 1614, in which the Nayaks of Thanjavur, and the Nayaks of Madurai and Jinji were ranged on opposing sides (the latter espoused the cause of the usurper). Thanjavur's protégé was ultimately successful; but the ascent of Venkatapati Raya meant only a temporary ceasefire. Warfare did not cease totally, for the Nayak of Madurai continued to be engaged in attempts to enlarge his territory at the cost of the Thevar of Ramnad and the Nayak of Thanjavur, while also trying to resist the encroachment of Mysore into his own land. It was also at this time that, taking advantage of the problems in the southern part of the peninsula, the Deccani Sultanates began their move southwards. At that time, the political situation in south India was reported to be extremely volatile, full of 'great troubles and broyles ..., both homebred and foreign ...' .[4]

The 1630s saw the southward expansion of the Mughal Empire, and Bijapur and Golconda signed the Deed of Submission to Shah Jahan in

1636. The Mughals did not make any further attempts to enter the Deccan in any major way until late in the reign of Aurangzeb, but following this submission, Bijapur and Golconda turned their attention southwards. Thereafter, the records are replete with accounts of the movement of armies. In 1642, part of the territory of the Nayak of Armagon was conquered by Bijapur, and the English were sure that the 'Moores' would 'have all this country ere many years; for what with the King of Vizapore on one side and the King of Gulquondah on the other, the Gentues themselves being divided among themselves, it is even impossible that their country can continue'.[5]

The entry of the Deccani Sultanates did not by any means signal an end to the internal strife in Vijayanagar; on the contrary, it just gave the king yet another enemy to deal with. The last king of the Vijayanagar Empire, Sriranga III, ascended the throne in 1642, and was immediately involved in wars with his Nayaks. In that year, he marched south at the head of an army. Tirumala Nayak of Madurai formed an alliance with Vijayaraghava Nayak of Thanjavur and the Nayak of Jinji, but Thanjavur later went over to Sriranga's side. Initial successes for this alliance led Tirumala Nayak to appeal to Golconda for help,[6] and the Golconda troops besieged the capital, Vellore. Sriranga, for his part, appealed to Bijapur, who provided help in exchange for '15 lacke of pagothaes and 24 elephants'.[7]

The armies of Bijapur and Golconda now extended their operations in the south, and in 1644, Pulicat was besieged by the Golconda troops. The Nayak of Jinji began to advance with the intention of joining Golconda, but Sriranga recalled his general Krishnappa Nayak (who was at the time engaged in operations against Jinji)[8] and sent him against the Golconda troops outside Pulicat. Krishnappa Nayak fell on the besieging army, 'and put the Moores to flight beyond Armagon, where they are now gathering a head againe … .'[9]

Sriranga initially met with success in his efforts, but in 1646, there was a joint invasion by Bijapur and Golconda, with Mir Jumla leading the latter's forces. Mir Jumla quickly gained possession of the areas around Pulicat, as well as the fortress of Udayagiri, before marching further south. The Nayak of Thanjavur purchased peace,[10] but the Nayak of Madurai concluded an alliance with Bijapur, and marched to Jinji at the head of a combined army. However, Golconda, then engaged in the siege of Jinji, now came to an agreement with Bijapur, and, handing over the siege to Bijapur, retired northwards. Jinji fell in 1649 to Bijapur. Vellore, the Vijayanagar capital, had fallen to Golconda a year earlier, and with that, the Vijayanagar Empire came to an end. Sriranga was forced to flee, and finally found shelter in Mysore. The erstwhile empire was now divided between Golconda and Bijapur, with Golconda seizing those areas 'of the coast of Coromandel, which lay conveniently for him; and the King of Bijapur, having taken what lay next to him, pursued his conquest as far as the Cape of Negapatam'.[11]

The end of the Vijayanagar Empire did not, however, mean an end to the wars, for Bijapur and Golconda now began to dispute the division of the spoils.[12] In 1653, the fortress of Penukonda was taken by Bijapur's troops. Mir Jumla, alarmed at the success of Bijapur, now tried to instigate the Raja of Mysore to attack Bijapur. Sriranga, who had taken refuge in Mysore, attempted to take advantage of this development to return to his empire, and was (again) initially quite successful. He managed to recapture many of the districts near Madras, with the exception of Poonamallee; this was probably easier for him to do, as by this time (1656), Mir Jumla had defected to the Mughals. In November 1656, Sriranga besieged Pulicat, 'where 'tis said most of the Nabob's riches are stowed'.[13] Sriranga's troops were led by Koneri Chetti, but in January 1657, he (Koneri Chetti), came to an agreement with Mir Jumla's lieutenant, Tupaki Krishnappa Nayak and abandoned the siege. Sriranga's troops were defeated, but now Golconda's troops entered the arena against Tupaki Krishnappa Nayak. Later in October 1658, Tupaki Krishnappa Nayak's forces were defeated by Golconda's troops, led by Quli Beg (later Neknam Khan). In 1659, Bijapur once again marched south, and captured Thanjavur. Sriranga lost what little he had managed to regain, and retired once again to Mysore.

Thus, from 1642–59, there was more or less continuous warfare, 'with parties of both sides in all places', and with 'sometimes the one, sometime the other party [proving] alternately victorious, and between them both draw a miserable ruine on the country . . .' .[14] Even the final defeat and disappearance of the Vijayanagar Empire and the establishment of Bijapur and Golconda rule did not signal an end to war, for the conflict between Madurai, Thanjavur and Mysore continued. In 1660–1, Madurai invaded Thanjavur. In 1663, Bijapur invaded Madurai, and besieged Trichi (modern Thiruchirapalli) with Thanjavur's help. The Nayak of Madurai (Chokkanatha Nayak) purchased peace, and, in turn, marched on Thanjavur.

In 1672, Abul Hasan Qutb Shah, the last of the Golconda Sultans, ascended the throne. The following year saw the resumption of hostilities between Madurai and Thanjavur. Thanjavur was invaded once again in 1673, and was finally defeated, and the Nayak, Vijayaraghava, was killed.[15] Chokkanatha, Nayak of Madurai, installed his foster brother as the new Nayak of Thanjavur,[16] but he soon revolted, and asserted his independence. Vijayaraghava's son appealed to Bijapur for help, and Ekoji, Shivaji's half-brother, was sent to Thanjavur. In 1676, he usurped the throne to establish the Maratha kingdom of Thanjavur. Thanjavur remained technically subordinate to Bijapur, even if it was in fact an independent kingdom. In the course of these decades, Golconda acquired control of most of the Coromandel Coast. A small section around Jinji remained under Bijapur until 1677–8, after which it was captured by the Marathas under Shivaji. By 1678, therefore, there were two Maratha kingdoms in the south; one at

Jinji, and the other at Thanjavur, controlling the Kaveri delta. Further to the south was an area nominally under the Nayak of Madurai, but actually under their former subordinates, the Setupatis of Ramnad. The European companies had settlements dotted along the coast, within the territories of all these separate powers, and had to deal with them both on the coast itself, and in the interior, in the cloth manufacturing areas.

Abul Hasan's reign also saw the rise to power of the Brahman brothers, Madanna and Akkanna. Madanna was reported to have begun his career as a *sarraf*, and later became the secretary of Syed Muzaffar, who was made the Mir Jumla in 1672.[17] Later, Syed Muzaffar was replaced as the Mir Jumla by Madanna himself. Madanna then instituted a policy of appointing his own relatives to high posts in the government. To start with, his brother Akkanna was put in charge of the army. Then, in 1675, Madanna took the farm of the southern part of the Golconda Sultanate, and appointed a relative, Podili Lingappa, as *tarafdar* of Poonamallee.

While much is made of Madanna's policy, it is to be remembered that Brahmans had generally been part of the government earlier, too, and not just in the Golconda Sultanate. For instance, two Brahman brothers, Venkata and Kanappa, were the *adigars* at Madras, and they managed to gain enough favour with the English to temporarily oust the Chief Merchant, Sesadri Chetti.[18] At about the same time, Mir Jumla's personal secretary was reported to be a Brahman. Later in the century, in connection with the Marathas of Jinji, one frequently comes across the name of Gopal Pandit, the 'chiefest man' of the Maratha ruler of Jinji. On the other hand, what emerged under Madanna was apparently a deliberate policy of promoting Brahmans over others. This aroused the hostility of the established nobility of Golconda. Tangentially, the efficiency with which the rents were collected, as well as the limitations sought to be enforced on trade, especially at Madras, resulted in the animosity of the English as well. It is perhaps this last which has led to so much being said about the system of tax farming in Golconda. While accepting the fact that Golconda was the wealthiest of the southern kingdoms, there is always the implication that this wealth was also the result of exploitative tax farming practices. In the post-1674 period, under the leadership of Madanna, the mechanics of tax farming were probably systematized, so as to be much more visible, as well as more efficient, from the govemment's point of view. However, it was not yet the sign of an impending collapse of the economy or the state, with everyone out to grab as much of the wealth as possible. On the contrary, the system set in place by Madanna probably formed the basis of the Mughal settlement after the conquest, as J.F. Richards has pointed out.[19] At the beginning of the seventeenth century, it was probably this systematization which allowed the alliance between Golconda and the Marathas, a link between the wealthiest and the most warlike of the southern powers.

The rise of the Marathas under Shivaji brought a new element into the politics of the Deccan. The Marathas had arrived on the Coromandel Coast with the Bijapur army early in the seventeenth century, but they became an important force only after the 1670s, when the conflict between the Nayaks of Madurai and Thanjavur escalated. At about the same time, in Maharashtra, Shivaji was crowned the Chhatrapati. Shivaji's raids had initially been directed at the Bijapur kingdom; but before long, the raids had also taken him into the Mughal Empire. In the south, despite the fact that the Marathas had entered the region with the Bijapuri army, it still seemed reasonable to apply to Bijapur for help, whether against Golconda or, as happened later, against Madurai. Mention has already been made of the invasion of Thanjavur by Chokkanatha Nayak. The widow of the Thanjavur Nayak escaped with her son to the safety of the Dutch settlement of Nagapattinam, and appealed to Bijapur for help. The Sultan sent Ekoji, Shivaji's half-brother, on an expedition, in the course of which the Nayak placed by Madurai on the Thanjavur throne (Alagiri Nayak), was defeated. The son of the late Nayak, Chengmaladas, was placed on the throne. However, in 1676, when the Adil Shahi Sultan died, Ekoji usurped the throne to establish the Maratha kingdom of Thanjavur.

In 1674, the year Chengmaladas was installed on the throne, Shivaji had himself crowned as an orthodox Hindu king, in a well-orchestrated and carefully conceived ceremony.[20] Shortly after this, Madanna, the Brahman minister of Abul Hasan Qutb Shah, persuaded the Golconda king to enter into an alliance with Shivaji. According to this, Golconda was to send 1,00,000 *hun* every year to the Marathas,[21] in exchange for which the kingdom was to be secured from Maratha raids. In 1677 came the next stage of this alliance, when Abul Hasan subsidized Shivaji's Karnataka expedition. The idea was that Shivaji would march through Golconda to Thanjavur and Bijapur's possessions along the coast, and after conquering those areas, he would hand them over to Golconda.[22]

The factors at Fort St. George reported that Shivaji was 'entertained in the King of Golcondas service', and had marched through the country 'with an army of 20 million Horse and 40 million Foot'. The vanguard of this army was reported in May 1677 to be at Kanchipuram, 'about 4 leagues Gentu hence'.[23] Fort St. George was kept in a state of readiness to repel any possible attack by Shivaji, but the latter made no such attempt, and merely wrote asking for some supplies to be sent to him.[24] It was considered important to retain Shivaji's friendship, for his power was reported to be increasing, and he exercised 'so much authority in the King of Gulcondahs Country, that he sends about to receive the Kings Rents by his own people'.[25] However, this desire did not include supplying him with 'Ingeniers', as this would result in 'encreasing his power, [and] rendering both Golconda and the Moghull our Enemys . . .' .[26]

In accordance with the Golconda alliance, Shivaji marched towards Jinji, the centre of Bijapuri control on the coast. The fortress there was captured without much delay, but instead of handing it over to Golconda, Shivaji kept it, to establish the second centre of Maratha power in the south. Jinji continued to be attached to the parent kingdom in Maharashtra (unlike Thanjavur, which was conceived, and existed as, an independent kingdom), and became more important as a Maratha stronghold at the end of the century, when Rajaram fled there for sanctuary. Jinji remained in Maratha hands until it was captured by the Mughals.

Having captured Jinji, Shivaji marched towards Thanjavur, but then came to an agreement with Ekoji, by which he 'delivered back to Eccogee a good part of the Country worth 2 Lacks of Pardoes per Annum which [he] had taken from him, and Eccogee in lieu thereof had paid 3 Lacks of Pardoes in ready money . . . .'[27] Later in the same year, Shivaji was reported to be in the vicinity of Kanchipuram, 'whereupon the inhabitants were put into great feares, thinking that the Towne would be taken and plundered, and they reported alsoe that those Horse with other forces were intended to proceed further into the King of Gulcondahs country, and to take Pullimelle Castle . . .' . The report proved to be false, for the troops were actually engaged in the siege of Vellore. Shortly afterwards, Abdullah Khan, commandant of Vellore Fort, surrendered to Shivaji, so that 'Sevagee by his Deputys [had] a full and quiett possession of all those countrys about those two strong Castles of holds of Chenge and Veloor . . .' .[28]

Meanwhile in 1681, Prince Akbar rebelled against Aurangzeb, and fled south to take shelter at Sambhaji's court. There already existed an alliance between the Marathas and Golconda, which, though strained by Shivaji's refusal to give up Jinji, nevertheless still existed. Aurangzeb could not afford the possibility that Akbar, supported by the Marathas and Golconda, would gain control of the Deccan. As he was aware, that (i.e. control of the Deccan) had been the route that he himself had followed to the throne. The Deccan and its problems therefore became of immediate concern, and in 1682, the Emperor's court moved to Aurangabad. Aurangzeb spent the remainder of his reign in the Deccan.

In 1685, the Mughal army moved into Bijapur, which fell a year later. Thereafter operations against Golconda began. During the campaign against Bijapur, a message from Abul Hasan to the Marathas had been intercepted, making plans for concerted action against the Mughals.[29] Shah Alam (later Bahadur Shah I) was sent to begin operations against Golconda. At the Battle of Malkhed, the Golconda army was defeated; the commander-in-chief of the Golconda troops, Muhammad Ibrahim, defected to the Mughals.[30] Abul Hasan left Hyderabad to retire into the fortress of Golconda. The official reason for the attack on Golconda was that Abul Hasan had 'made his vagabond Hindus the managers and administrators of the affairs of State', and that the Persians (i.e. the Shias) 'began to practise there publicly all kinds of shameful sins ...' .[31] Equally important, of course, was the fact of the alliance with the Marathas, and the non-payment of tribute to the Mughals. (This last was according to the terms of the Deed of Submission to Shah Jahan.)

In 1686, Madanna and Akkanna were murdered in Golconda Fort. This removed the two main 'managers and administrators' but did not end the Mughal threat, and on 14 January 1687, Aurangzeb's troops marched into the kingdom; shortly after, the siege of Golconda Fort began.[32] In May 1687, Shaikh Nizam, commander of the Golconda forces outside the fort, defected to the Mughals, and finally, on 21 September, after a siege of 'eight months and a few days',[33] the fort fell.

News of the taking of Golconda Fort and the imprisonment of Abul Hasan reached Madras in October 1687. Aurangzeb appointed Qasim Khan (later Ali Asghar Khan) as the first Mughal *faujdar* of the Karnatak. Qasim Khan was a former Golconda official, as was Mahabat Khan, the first Mughal governor. Khan was reported to have arrived with 10,000 men to the 'Chengie country, to warr against those parts'.[34] Another former Golconda official, Fateh Khan, was confirmed as governor of Chingleput, while 'Madanna Anta Puntolo and Sanganna' were restored to their former positions as governors of Kanchipuram and Poonamallee.[35]

Thus it appeared that the Mughal conquest did not send any immediate signals of drastic change, for many of the old officials continued. Of the Europeans, the English were the most apprehensive, for they were already involved in a conflict with the Mughals in Bengal. The Dutch and the French were reported to have gone to the Mughal camp, 'to congratulate his conquest'. It was decided that, as an initial measure, the English would write to 'our friend Nabob Mahobat Cawn, ... to congratulate the Mogulls conquest of the Fort & Country, and to offer our Services to him ...' .[36] The fact that Golconda officials were able to continue was, however, a purely temporary phase. From December 1687 they began to be transferred to other parts of the Empire.[37] Ruhullah Khan, the chief *bakshi* of the Empire, became the new governor. The Mughals divided the former Golconda kingdom into two parts, comprising the *suba* of Hyderabad and that of the Karnataka. The latter had its headquarters at Kanchipuram, from where the attacks on the Marathas were organized. By 1689, therefore, the arena of warfare had once again moved to the coast. In 1690, Ali Mardan Khan was appointed *faujdar* of the Karnatak. Technically subordinate to the *subedar* of Hyderabad, he was actually equal in status, and reported directly to the court. Rather ineffectual in his official capacity, Ali Mardan Khan also became the first Mughal official to be kidnapped by the Marathas. He was held prisoner for two years, and was finally released only after the payment of a large sum as ransom.

Maratha attacks on the south had begun in 1687, with the end of the Golconda kingdom and their alliance. From 1690, the Mughal-Maratha conflict centred on the fortress of Jinji. Zulfiqar Khan, son of the *wazir* of the Empire, was put in charge of the siege of Jinji. In May 1691, Kam Baksh was 'sent to put down the rebels of the country of Jinji and to root out the enemy who ruled there'.[38] The Mughal-Maratha conflict was reported to have 'so alarm'd the Country, that most of the Inhabitants have left Conjeveron & the other great Townes, to secure their persons & estates, from their violence …' .[39]

In 1696, Maratha and Mughal troops were reported to be near Fort St. David; the Marathas were reported to be at Tiruvadi, when Daud Khan arrived 'with about 3,000 choice horse'. The Marathas fled 'and the Moors resettled'.[40] Jinji finally fell to the Mughal forces in 1698 after a nine-year siege; the 'hundred other forts which make up the kingdom of the Karnataka with some ports of the Europeans, were annexed to the empire. . . . The conquered fort was named Nusratgarh'.[41]

The coastal areas, naturally, did not remain unaffected by the problems. But, in the decade before the vanishing of the Golconda Sultanate, there had been a certain degree of peace, i.e. there was no widespread movement of armies. Problems did occur, for the local officials placed frequent hindrances in the way of trade, and the English began to make serious efforts to find a place outside Golconda. This had to be in the 'Gingee country'. Desultory attempts had been made to establish a factory in this part of the coast even earlier, as, for example, at Devanamapattinam around the 1640s. In 1674, Nasir Muhammad Khan of Jinji offered to allow the English to settle factories 'at or near Porto Novo, and at Vardavur neare Polichery and to make forts …' .[42] The offer was considered very seriously, not, at that time, so much because of the possible threat from the Indian rulers, but because of the proximity of the French (at San Thomé) and the Dutch (at Pulicat), and the possibility of English trade at Madras being affected thereby. No immediate result ensued, but from the 1680s, the matter began to be pursued more vigorously.

In 1684, the Court of Directors at London decided to write to the president of their factory at Surat. The idea was that he would contact Sambhaji, 'to press him to give you a speedy and favourable dispatch in that your demand of liberty to build a ffort in his Country …' .[43] In 1685, it was decided to dissolve the factory at Masulipattinam, on account of 'the nearness of Madapollam and Pettipolee'.[44] Two years later, all the three factories were dissolved, 'by reason of the Warrs & troubles in those parts, and danger of the Mogulls forces …' .[45] The English derived some consolation from the fact that the Jinji area was still trouble-free. The Dutch had the same benefit, far from the 1660s, they had increasingly begun to concentrate their attention on the far south, from their headquarters at

Nagapattinam. This port was also in Maratha territory, for it was in the Thanjavur kingdom.

The seventeenth century was clearly a turbulent one. The English factors were, at the end to the century, ordered by the Court of Directors to:

> keep fair with all parties and side with none without absolute necessity and if yt happens be sure to engage no further than yt you may Secure your retreat and have a fair excuse is afterwards question'd for it: yt what you did was ye effect of meere necessity not choice, yt warr and bloodshed are inconsistent with ye Essence of a merchant. . . .[46]

'Warr and Bloodshed' were, no doubt, incompatible with continued trade: but the merchants had to deal with such political disturbances and still pursue their trade. This meant dealing not just with the problems caused by insecurity, but also with the multiple levels of state machinery, for income, both for the state and for the individual, had to be derived wherever possible—and very often, this meant through the merchants. The East India Companies no doubt provided a means of garnering income, not just because of the volume of their trade, but also because, as outsiders, they had to get concessions from the state authorities in order to establish any kind of base for trade.

Relations between the Companies and the state were very often characterized by extortion. Masulipattinam was the first destination for both the Dutch and the English. There were definite advantages to settling in there—since it was the chief port of the Golconda Sultanate, and occupied a position similar to Surat on the west coast. It was the centre of a major textile producing region, and was also well connected overland. The importance of Masulipattinam was recognized early, for the English factors reported that the 'welth and welfare of the kingdome of Gulcondah' lay in its 'inland manyfactures, which findes most or all his vent by sea transporte, shipped the most part by the Moores and the least part by the Cristians . . .' .[47]

However, merchants at Masulipattinam also had to face a great many hindrances to trade. The Governor of Masulipattinam was a royal official, but one who had bid for the appointment, i.e. a revenue farmer. The usual pattern was, apparently, of one person taking up a farm, and then subletting it to others, so that any person who could 'devise a newe course of raysinge newe revenues'[48] was very welcome. One such 'newe' source was obviously the European merchants.

In 1620–1, a new governor was appointed, who had taken the farm of Masulipattinam for '15,000 pagodas per annum more then his predecessor'. He farmed out the monopoly of 'buying, selling and changing all gould and silver brought into this porte' to one *sarraf*, with the result that the English could not 'put of our ryalls but as that onely sharoffe please to take them . . . ' .[49] This attempt led to concerted action by the English, Dutch and the local merchants, so that after about three months, the monopoly 'fell of itselfe'.[50]

This was the first, and probably the only, instance in which Indian and foreign merchants came together, in the seventeenth century, to resist the obstacles placed by state machinery in the path of trade; and the one thing of which there was no shortage was obstacles. Later, in the early 1620s, the English complained that they had been 'discorraged' from the trade of Masulipattinam by the 'unsufferable abuses' of Mahmud Taqi, the former governor and the then governor, who had 'infringed our previlege and the antient custom of the land'.[51] They submitted a list of their demands, including (1) the liberty to trade at Masulipattinam without 'abridgment', and (2) that the Governor should not detain their goods. If he wanted to purchase any, then he should 'bargaine in his own house, according to reason and custom of merchants'.[52]

One solution that the Europeans found was to leave Masulipattinam and find another place where perhaps they would be welcomed, and have better trading conditions. The Dutch had not wasted time about this, for they established their base at Pulicat as early as 1612. The English began their search for an alternative location soon after their arrival at Masulipattinam, for, as they pointed out to their superiors at London, one of the main reasons for Dutch success was their possession of a fort at Pulicat. A brief attempt was made to share Pulicat with the Dutch, but this came to nothing. The English then decided on Armagon, near Pulicat—in fact, at the northern end of the same lake on which Pulicat stood. The English moved to Armagon in the 1620s, shortly after they lost their settlement at Amboyna. It was believed that, as Armagon lay outside the Golconda Sultanate, they would be relatively free there, for they would be able to deal with the local Nayak on terms of greater equality than were possible in Golconda. Besides, in a smaller place, there would probably be fewer levels of bureaucracy to deal with, and therefore less trouble with local officials, especially if they managed to reach an agreement with the head.

The English did not find Armagon to be all that much better, for the Nayak there was found to be unfriendly. Shortly before the move to Madras in 1639–40, the English reported that Armagon 'affords nothing of itself, not so much as a peece of white Cloath but comes from other places: as for Merchants, how misserable poor they are, by the Nagues continuall forceings . . . ' .[53] Again, one of the reasons for the move to Madras was to get away from Golconda's control. However, it did not remedy matters for any length of time, for, as mentioned earlier, before very long, the frontiers of Golconda had expanded to include the area around Madras. Mir Jumla's forces blockaded Madras between September 1657 and April 1658, while Neknam Khan blockaded, it in 1666.[54] But the worst, and most constant, hindrances came close to a decade later, after 1674, when Madanna and Akkanna became Golconda's ministers. In 1675, Madanna took the farm of the southern part of the Golconda Sultanate, and appointed a relative, Podili Lingappa, as *tarafdar* of Poonamallee. Lingappa's name is, thereafter, consistently mentioned in connection with hindering the trade at Madras.

In 1678, Lingappa wrote to a chief merchant at Madras, Kasi Viranna, 'threatening to doe this Towne all ye mischief at Court that possible he could if he did not lend him a sum of mony'. In another letter, Lingappa informed Viranna that 'he had sent his Men for all the Sharofs and Coyners of this Towne with all the chops and Stamps for pagodas to be brought away to him Imediately'. Viranna wrote back that the *sarrafs* and coiners in the mint were the Company's servants, for the English had minting facilities at Madras even 'before this country fell under ye Kings of Gulcondah'. Therefore, Lingappa had no rights over them.[55]

In 1679, all the corn coming into Madras was stopped. Lingappa's response to a letter on the subject was 'much Corne of Pullimelee to be sold, & the Kings occasions requiring the mony, if we would furnish 7000 pagodas to supply the want, they would take off the stopp'.[56] Lingappa next tried to fix the price at which paddy was to be sold in the markets of Madras. The then governor, Streynsham Master, declared that the market was 'free to all men to buy and sell in', that no one could be forced to sell their goods at fixed rates, and 'if it should please God to make it dearer or chaper 'twas not in the power of a man to alter what God Almighty had decreed . . .' .[57] Lingappa was also reported to have taken up the farm of San Thomé, earlier in Viranna's hands, for the same sum that Viranna had paid. In 1680, he placed an embargo on all the cloth coming into Madras. Again, in 1681, he placed an embargo on all goods and provisions coming into Madras, forbidding the 'Country people to carry anything to Towne'.[58] At this time, it was decided to try to get permission to set up a fort and factory in the 'Chengy Country which is out of the Gulcondah Dominions', for this would prevent 'Lingappa or any other Soobidar of this Country from being capable of spoiling al our business'. The Dutch on the coast were more successful than the English precisely because they had numerous factories, 'which being divided into severall governments, if they be obstructed in their business by one Governour they have another place to friend . . .'.[59]

In 1684, when Lingappa had been the *tarafdar* long enough to be a constant thorn in the flesh of the English, the factors were told that, if absolutely necessary, they could take strong action, to make the 'Governors . . . sensible of Our power'.[60] Soldiers were to be sent out from England for the better defence of the Company's settlements on the coast, and if any further problems were encountered, then the factors were to inform the Golconda authorities that Madras had 'cost the Company 300,000 pounds Sterling; when they will reimburse the Company that Sume, You will move us to accept it & give them the ffort & towne ...' .[61] However, this could be done only if the factors successfully established a base in the Jinji territory. The underlying reason was the same as the one that inspired the English to move out of Golconda in the first place—that Jinji did not have the kind of state structure that Golconda did, and would perforce give more freedom of action to the English. In one way, this can be compared to the English encouragement of trade at Madras—that they would at least get the customs duties; the same logic would apply to a smaller kingdom. In the case of Golconda, control of the source of the income, the fort, was necessary.

For the Mughals, too, the concern was the same. Within the Empire, the Mughals had never allowed fortifications, for they did not see any need for merchants to defend themselves when the state was there to do it for them. The Europeans, for their part, believed that the fortifications were necessary precisely against that state, for it was seen as encroaching, obstructive and oppressive, and so, detrimental to the interests of European trade. From the Indian point of view, what was being done was, if successful, beneficial to the Indian merchants, for it would once again place the Indian and European merchants on an equal footing. It is in this context that one must see Sa'adatullah Khan's attempts to establish a port on the Coromandel Coast. Unfortunately, the conquest of Golconda, followed, very shortly, but the disintegration of the Mughal Empire, led to smaller kingdoms, who could not exercise even a limited degree of control. More important, it led to an extremely fluid situation, in which there were constant movements, not of armies, but of armed raiders, not excluding the Marathas, who increased the dependence on the secure European fort.

The records show that there were several obstacles in the way of the Indian merchants. In an account submitted in 1690, by the Kunimedu merchants of the English Company for the poor quality cloth that they had supplied, the merchants declared that they had had their contract well in hand, 'but the Mogulls visiting these parts, together with the Sadd mortality and famine put a great Check thereto, by the weavers going to other places . . .' . In addition, 'Severall weavers ran away with our mony, so that every way we are losers'. Such uncertain conditions would naturally make them more wary of risking their own money, and so, the tendency would be to gravitate towards those who would provide them with money. Supplying cloth to the Companies meant, first, that they did not have to tie up large sums of their own money, and second, that with the protection of the Company's name, they could, perhaps, trade on their own account as well. For the Company's trade, they could, when necessary, claim more advances; for instance, when the merchants at Sadraspattinam and Tevnepattinam complained to the Dutch about their losses, 'they forthwith advanced them

15%, notwithstanding which they could perform their Contract, whereupon the Dutch ordered them to desist from any further provideing . . .' .[62]

In the seventeenth century, this was the major advantage that the European companies had—that they were able to negotiate with the local governments on fairly equal terms. Given seventeenth century conditions, therefore, security of both trade and person was to be had only in the vicinity of the European forts. The volume of trade that the Companies controlled, and therefore the amount of revenue that they could generate, was far in excess of the individual Indian merchants, who no longer had the support of the guild. While initially the Indian merchant had been able to mobilize State support, the increasing political instability made this support (or its possibility) steadily more inaccessible. Equally important, the absorption of Golconda into the Mughal Empire led naturally, to both, a shift in centres of power, as well as centres of legitimacy. The Mughal emperor was a distant figure, both mentally and physically, and the new state structure was one to which the merchants had to adjust. However, they did not have the time to make this adjustment. The collapse of the new structure before the establishment (of the system and the access to power within the system), together with the increasing tendency to localization and regionalization, provided the base for increased rivalry among the European powers, to consolidate their hold. Here too, the Indian merchant was rather worse off than the Europeans, for he often lacked the resources to get access to the new courts. So, once again, it made more sense to link their fortunes with the Europeans.

This last, of linking with the Europeans, and taking advantage of the income that they generated, was the other aspect of relations between the Companies and the Indian states. Going by the records, it is very tempting to argue that there was a permanent state of armed (or semi-armed) neutrality that existed, with each side constantly trying to assert its independence of action, and the other challenging it. Though all were in a sense prepared to defend themselves, should the occasion have arisen, by having a small force of soldiers, they were used only when absolutely necessary. However, they were on all accounts to remain outside local politics. But relations were quite as often cordial, and very often, the rulers welcomed the Europeans.

It is to be remembered that Asia was familiar with the spectacle of groups of merchants settling down in a place and counry not their own. Arab settlements were to be found in Indian ports, while Indian and Chinese settlements flourished in the Malay Archipelago. According to W.H. Moreland,[63] foreign traders enjoyed a kind of 'extraterritoriality' long before the arrival of the Europeans. At Malacca, the Portuguese found settlements of Chinese and Indian merchants, while at Calicut, they found Arab and Egyptian merchants. These communities apparently enjoyed the right to follow their own laws and customs, and 'each nation had a chief or headman of its own, who exercised the functions of a governor in regard to his nationals'.[64] Duarte Barbosa reported that, when any merchant arrived at Calicut, the king 'assigned him a Nayre [Nair, but probably used here in the sense of agent], to protect and serve him, and a Chetie [Chetti] clerk to keep his accounts and look after his affairs, and a broker to arrange for him to obtain such goods as he had need of . . . '.[65] On the east coast, this may not have been the pattern followed, for the sources that we have do not mention such practices, at least in such clear terms. On the other hand, numerous local rulers made direct overtures to the Europeans. For instance, in 1622, the Nayak of Thanjavur suggested that the English could settle in his dominions, saying that they could buy 'pepper and anything the land doth afford, and likewise buye those commodities that they [the English] doe bring with them, as tine, leade, iron and redd cloth ... '.[66] He gave them the choice of living under his protection, as the Portuguese had been doing, of 'to fortifie as the Danes have done' at Tranquebar.[67] In 1608, Krishnappa Nayak of Jinji gave the Dutch permission to build a fort at Devanamapattinam. However, Portuguese influence at the Vijayanagar court put paid to the Dutch plans.[68] Later, in 1610, in an agreement of the Dutch with the Vijayanagar king, Venkata, they got exclusive rights to Pulicat, for other Europeans were not allowed to live and trade there.[69] Two years on, they were allowed to build a fortress there. Devanamapattinam eventually became the site of the English Company's Fort St. David.

In the case of the Nayak of Madurai, though the Europeans were welcomed, they were, in general, not allowed to build fortifications. In 1658, after the capture of Nagapattinam, two Dutch officials were deputed to the Nayak's court, to try and get a grant for exclusive rights to the pearl fishery, in return for payment of a toll of 2 per cent. Their demands included: no other Europeans were to be allowed to trade in the Bay of Madurai, pepper was to be brought in only on Dutch ships, the Dutch were to be given preference in the purchase of rice, and lastly, permission was to be got for the building of a fort at Tuticorin.[70] The Nayak categorically refused to accept these proposals.[71] The Dutch could only succeed in their monopolistic efforts at the end of the century, when the Nayak was too weak to enforce his orders, and moreover needed Dutch support against the Thevar of Ramnad. At about this time, the Nayak sent letters inviting the English to settle within his kingdom, and said that 'much pepper' was available there. The English did not take him up on his offer.[72] A similar overture had been made earlier, by 'the Cawn of Chengie Nasir Mahmud Cawn'. The English took serious consideration of this offer in view of the 'great troubles' because of the Dutch and the 'Inconvenient Neighbourhood of the French'. No decision was actually taken, but options were left open; a letter and a 'present' sent to Jinji.[73] The idea was dropped when the French left San Thomé for Pondicherri.

In 1634, the English received the so-called 'Golden Farman' for trade in the kingdom of Golconda. This remitted customs on 'such goods and horses as the English shall bring for their Companies accompt', and stated that the *farman* had been granted because the Sultan's subjects 'have commerce' with the English.[74] Another *farman* granted in 1639, was more or less a repetition of the Golden Farman.

In 1639, they got the grant of Madras from Nayak Damarla Venkatadri (or Venkatapati), the ruler of Kalahasti, who ruled the coast from Pulicat to San Thomé. The grant gave 'full power and authority to governe and dispose of the Goverment of Madraspatam for the terme and space of two yeares . . . '. Thus all goods either imported or exported by the English were to be completely free of customs duty, and they were to pay half the regular inland tolls. In addition, they were granted the right to mint coins in Madras.[75] The grant was renewed in 1645 by Sriranga. The reasons ascribed to the Nayak for the grant were that he wanted his country to 'flurrish and grow rich', which was possible only through trade; and he hoped that the fort, once built, would shelter him from his enemies, if necessary.[76] Later in the century, when the English were trying to move into the 'Chengy country', they entered into a treaty with Rajaram, the Maratha king. The English purchased the 'Fort of Tevnepatam, with al its gunns, buildings etc. necessaryes ..., as also the ground Woods and Rivers round the said Fort within the random Shott of a greate Gunn...' for the sum of 'fourty thousand Chuckraes' (*chakrams*, the local coin). The grant further stated that the fort was to be 'soly under the disposure of the English Company and noe other whatsoever and that neither the Duan, Soldiers, Avaldars or any other Governours or Officers, Shall upon any pretence whatever have anything to Say or doe within the said fort or ground . . . '. As in the case of Madras, the government of the town was now totally in the hands of the English; here too, they got the right to mint coins. Unlike the earlier grant, however, this specifically said that the king would 'assist and defend them in the quiett and free Possession [of the fort], from ye French and all other European Nation or others . . . '.[77]

Other European companies in turn also came to an agreement with the local rulers. The French had been the last of the Europeans to come to India, in 1672. They first established themselves at San Thomé, near Madras, a place where, according to Thévenot, chintz 'much finer and of better colours than anywhere else in India'[78] was made. However, they did not stay in possession of the place for any great length of time, for in 1674 they were defeated by the forces of Golconda, helped by the Dutch. Thereafter, forced to surrender and leave San Thomé, they came to an agreement with Sher Khan Lodi, the Bijapur Governor of the region, for the grant of Pondicherri.[79]

The treaty signed between Ekoji and the Dutch in 1676 also falls into the same pattern. This was probably the earliest of the agreements made by Ekoji after he became king. By this time, the Dutch were beginning to shift their base of operations from Pulicat to Nagapattinam, to try and exercise greater control over the Tuticorin coast and over Sri Lanka. This treaty ensured that the Dutch were given the privilege of paying only half the tax on exports from and imports into Thanjavur, as well as mint facilities in Nagapattinam; but the two seaports of Karaikal and Tirumalairajavirapattinam (which had been leased to the Dutch in 1674) were to revert to Ekoji.[80] It was at this time that the English stepped up efforts to set up a base in this area, searching for a place under the control of the Nayaks of Madurai or Jinji. I have already discussed the rather fruitless negotiations with the Nayak of Madurai. With Jinji, negotiations were begun shortly after the establishment of Maratha rule there. They dealt mainly with Harji Raja, the 'Chief Subidar' of the region, and his representative, Gopal Pandit, the Subedar of Porto Novo. The English wanted leave to settle at and trade from Porto Novo, Cuddalore and Kunimedu, which was granted in 1682. They further asked that lower customs rates be levied on their merchants; specifically, 'at Coomeed [Kunimedu] one per cent; at Cudaloor one, and three Eights; and at Porto Novo two, and one eight which together is one and a half per cent'. Also, they asked that they be free from 'other Petty troublesome Customes to Talliars, Concoplies and Pagothaes'.[81] For their part, Gopal Pandit and Harji Raja declared that the English were to come and settle at the seaport 'without feare', so that 'the Divan may receive greater and greater benefits'[82]—a statement strikingly reminiscent of the wishes attributed to Damarla Venkatadri at the time of the grant of Madras. Unfortunately for the English, they were not left to enjoy these benefits for very long, as the 1690s saw the spread of the Mughal-Maratha conflict to this region.

From 1687, major problems of relations with the Mughals began to arise. The Dutch were reported to have sided with the Mughals against Golconda, and the English were advised to give Golconda 'all the secret Countenance and advice in his affairs ... and assistance likewise underhand for his money ... so as ... wisely to improve the present advantage for ye Good of ye English Nation...' .[83]

The French were the first of the European Companies to reach a settlement with the Mughals, which they managed at a cost of Rs. 10,000 in 1688. In 1689, the Dutch got a favourable settlement—they were allowed to trade throughout the former Golconda Sultanate free of any tolls, land or sea custom, or market duties. Their earlier rights to mint coins and collect customs at Pulicat were also re-confirmed.[84]

It took a long time for the English to come to an agreement with the Mughals, for they were, to start off with, in a disadvantageous position, as a result of their problems with the Mughals in Bengal. However, relations between the two began to improve from 1689, and in 1690, the factors at Fort St. George were informed that arrangements were almost complete for a *farman* for Surat and Bengal. No agreement had been reached on Madras mainly because the negotiators did not have the exact terms of the earlier grants for Madras. It was therefore decided to send the two most favourable grants to the Mughal camp.[85] Their position was further strengthened when they supported the Mughal *faujdar*, Ali Asghar Khan, and later the commander of the Mughal army, Zulfiqar Khan, against the Marathas. The promised *farman* from Aurangzeb finally never arrived, but the English managed to establish cordial relations with the local authorities (Zulfiqar Khan, Asad Khan, Daud Khan Panni and others), and so were able to stabilize their position.

It was in December 1690 that the English got a *farman* from Zulfiqar Khan, confirming their possession of the

> Fort and Factory of Chinnapatam with accustomary Priveledges, the English Factorys of Metchlepatam, Madapollam Vizagapatam etc. within the territorys of Darullchard [*Dar-ul-Jehad*, or land of war] alias the Gulcondah Countrey, also their Settlements and Factorys of Dewnapatam, Eslamabad alias Cuddaloor, Mamood Bunder alias Porto Novo, Trimlevassull [Tirumalavasal] etc. Factorys within the territoryes of Chingee...[86]

The *farman*, however, was not followed to the letter, especially in the areas around Fort St. David. Mention has already been made of the bands of Marathas and the Mughal armies at Tiruvadi, near Fort St. David. The fall of Jinji did not change matters noticeably; instead, once again, attempts began to be made to gain control over the factories. It was reported that, after the fall of Jinji, the 'Aveldar' called the merchants and told them that if any of them had 'concerns in Cuddalore', they would be well advised 'to withdraw the same'.[87] Most of the problems were caused by Sulaiman Khan, who was said to have 'a desire to cause trouble to this place'[88] (i.e. Fort St. David). Between 18 and 26 February 1698, Sulaiman Khan attacked Cuddalore but he was beaten back. A little later, again in 1698, the factors reported that the losses suffered at Fort St. David were calculated as amounting to 1,04,397 pagodas. This sum included losses to the Company, to 'the Chuliars and other Black Merchants, to Committees, Chittees and Shroffs', as well as the losses incurred as a result of houses, gardens, paddy fields, cotton and cotton yarn being burnt.[89] Some attempts were made to resolve the problems, and Daud Khan sent one 'Ageesee Cawn' to settle matters, for he said that the attacks on the English were 'very prejudiciall to his Master's jaggeer'.[90]

In 1701, it was reported that of the 'five or six thousand weavers' that had settled near Fort St. David, there were only about 200 left. Some had, indeed, deserted as a result of the Mughal attacks, but many more had been drawn away by the French, so that Pondicherri now had between 1,500 and 2,000 weavers.[91] In the same year, the factors at Fort St. George complained that the Dutch, to 'engross the weavers', had deposited ten pagodas per loom as opposed to the customary five pagodas per loom.[92]

In 1702, Daud Khan was reported to have arrived at San Thomé 'with considerable forces of horse and foot ...' .[93] He besieged Madras for a while, and seized some of the Company's goods.[94] Daud Khan was reported to be acting in accordance with the *husbulhukum* of the Emperor, which accused the Europeans of taking on the role of pirates, rather than preventing piracies. This was, in fact, a major concern of the Mughals at this time, for Mughal ships on the Red Sea route were being attacked by pirates. The idea had long existed, that purchase of passes from the Europeans entitled those who had purchased them to the protection of the European ships, and thus, the Europeans were to be penalized for their failures in this respect. Here again, we see the continuation of the notion that had existed under Golconda—that the Europeans were merely additional players in the Asian markets, and their expertise was to be used while they were kept under control. Unfortunately, the local powers were now less able to exercise that control. In this instance, the English did not try to conciliate Daud Khan: rather, they sent him a letter saying that Madras could withstand a two-year siege 'besides the Sea open to us'.[95] At the same time, a letter was drafted to be sent to the other Europeans on the coast, saying that 'wee should find it our Interst to join and assist each other in this matter . . .' .[96] After the early seventeenth century joint action at Masulipattinam, this was the first proposal of any joint action—and significantly, it made no mention of any appeal to Indian merchants. The proposal, however, came to nothing, for the rivalry between the Europeans was too intense to permit any kind of joint action, even against a common threat.

In the long run, the Mughal invasion, and the subsequent Mughal-Maratha conflict, probably did more to increase the power of the European Companies than anything else. The Europeans had, of course, always been aware of the greater advantages that they would have in dealing with the smaller kingdoms, as can be seen in, for instance, the Dutch establishing themselves at Pulicat, and the English at Armagon and Madras. They were, therefore, wary of the Mughals when they first arrived in the south, particularly as they already had experience of the strength of the Mughals in the north. In both Surat and Bengal, the Europeans had not been allowed to fortify, and therefore, it appeared that the fate of the forts in the south too hung in the balance. However, before the consolidation of the conquest could take place, and the Mughal system of administration could be firmly established, Aurangzeb died. It has been pointed out that, in the initial stages, the Emperor's purpose was 'to mobilise, as completely as possible, funds that could be used for further aggressive expansion'.[97] This naturally meant that administration was a low priority, relegated to those on the scene, to manage as best they could. Aurangzeb's successors had less likelihood of succeeding, for they could not exercise even that degree of control, and so the Deccan continued to be left in the hands of the nobles. As in the past, with the representatives of Golconda, the Europeans did face obstacles, but the difference was that these obstacles could be dealt with at the local level itself, without reference to a higher authority. In the 1670s, when Lingappa was busy putting obstacles in the way of smooth trade in Madras, the factors complained of 'misgovernment at the helm', with a king who was more interested in pleasure than administration, but they were the last to deny that there was a state machinery that was in reasonably good working condition—enough, at any rate, to control them. By the 1690s, this had vanished. In 1698, the Mughal commander, Sulaiman Khan, was dissuaded from attacking Cuddalore (near Fort St. David) on the grounds that the 'English were now much stronger than formerly', and where, earlier, they kept to the Fort, they were now willing to march out to attack.[98] The beginnings of this demeanour can be traced back to 1678, when Streynsham Master declared that if necessary he would oppose by force Lingappa's attempt to fix the price at which paddy was sold.

To all this internal political turmoil was added an altogether different aspect, one that was not limited to the coast or to the south, but was common to all areas in which the Europeans traded—the rivalry between the Europeans. The Dutch, the entrants after the Portuguese, arrived to find that though Portuguese trade might have declined, Portuguese influence and presence definitely had not. In 1640, the English remarked that the presence of the Portuguese in their new settlement of Fort St. George, was likely to be useful for the growth of the settlement.[99] Earlier, they had used their influence to block Dutch efforts to set up a factory at Devanamapattinam,[100] a measure that was only a temporary success, for they did not succeed in preventing them from getting Pulicat. Thereafter, the Dutch successfully attacked and broke the Portuguese monopoly, capturing many of their strongholds, like Ormuz and Malacca. By 1656, the Portuguese possessions in Sir Lanka had been taken over, and in 1658, the last possession of the Portuguese on the Coromandel Coast, Nagapattinam, was also captured. With this, Portuguese power on the Coromandel Coast came to an end. Many Portuguese continued to live on the coast, but as private citizens rather than as members or representatives of an empire. While this aspect, i.e. of the private citizen/merchant, had become fairly well established even earlier,[101] it was confirmed by the Dutch conquests.

Of far more importance in our period was the Anglo-Dutch rivalry, which dominated much of the seventeenth century, and the Anglo-French rivalry, which began in the seventeenth century in a minor way, but steadily increased, to culminate in the well-documented Anglo-French wars of the eighteenth century. This European rivalry began in Asia and often exploded into wars in Europe. The effect of the wars fought in Europe were felt in Asia as well. War was not a regular or a necessary occurrence, but the rivalry was constant and took many forms.

Through most of the seventeenth century, Dutch trade was on a larger scale than that of either the English or the French.[102] The Portuguese introduced the system of cartazes, but it was the Dutch who used the cartaz much more effectively. In some cases, it was used to eliminate Asian shipping,[103] as happened along the stretch of coast between Tuticorin and Sri Lanka. More often, the cartaz was used as a means of redirecting shipping, so that Batavia had to be a port of call. In the first half of the seventeenth century, if Amsterdam was the re-export capital of the world, then it was not through lack of trying that the Dutch failed to make Batavia the re-export centre of Asia.

In addition to control of shipping, Dutch ships also participated directly in the trade of Asia, and consequently were far less dependent than the English on supplies of bullion from Europe. Quite apart from the European end of the enterprise, they also participated in the well-established Asian trade networks to a much larger extent than any of their other European competitors. A Dutch administrator, Jan Pietersz Coen, aptly described the nature of the Dutch participation when he said,

> Piece goods from Gujarat we can barter for pepper and gold on the coast of Sumatra, rials and cotton from the coast (Coromandel) for pepper in Bantam, sandalwood, pepper and rials we can barter for Chinese goods and Chinese gold; we can extract silver from Japan with Chinese goods, piece goods from the Coromandel coast in exchange for spices, other goods and gold from China, piece goods from Surat for spices and various other trifles—one thing leads to another. And all of it can be done without any money from the Netherlands and with ships alone.[104]

Dutch ships took a supply of textiles and spices to Japan, along with a few select European articles, which were sold for silver and, less often, for gold. Chinese silk was also acquired in exchange, and this, with the bullion, was used to make purchases in India. The English had no role to play in the Japan trade, for seventeenth-century Japan, under Tokugawa rule, had retreated into isolation. The Dutch were the only foreigners permitted in Japan, but they too were restricted to the artificial island of Deshima in the harbour of Nagasaki.

Despite their best efforts, the Dutch found that they could not monopolize the shipping of Asia. For one thing, there were far too many ports in India alone, and it was impossible to police all of them.[105] For another, while the Dutch ships were undoubtedly superior to the Asian ones, they were on par with those of the other Europeans. Too much interference with European shipping would have led to war, and then to disruption of trade, whether on a large or a small scale, which was something no one wanted. All the other Europeans also issued cartazes, and the pass finally came to indicate only which European Company was in charge of defending the ship to which the cartaz had been issued. Often, Asian shippers took cartazes from all the Companies, rather than risk getting into trouble.

As has been mentioned earlier, the Dutch made treaties with the local rulers, in which they specified exclusion of other Europeans. They also actively helped local rulers against the Europeans, as for example, between 1672 and 1674. At that time, the French had taken possession of San Thomé, and were besieged by the Golconda troops with Dutch help. Earlier too, the Dutch had helped their brokers, Malaya and Chinanna, with arms and ammunition, to be used for the Vijayanagar emperor. Helping with arms and ammunition was done at the time of the Mughal conquest also, for there were reports that Daud Khan had been supplied 'with powder and ammunition from Policat ...' .[106]

Anglo-Dutch rivalry could, and did, take many forms, not all of which were concerned with shipping. For instance, both the English and the Dutch had minting facilities, but it was noted that the Dutch made their pagodas 'finer than the Standard of the Country', which made them acceptable in more places than the English pagodas. This, according to the English, was not only 'for their own Conveniency, ... but to debase ours'.[107] It took almost another full decade before the English pagodas gained parity with the Dutch ones, '& in some places 1 per cent. better'. Problems however continued, for the Dutch 'malitiously endeavoured to depretiate them by advising Madana to coyn great quantities of our Stamp and Shape, but a fanam less in value ...' .[108]

While condemning the 'underhand' methods of the Dutch, the English nevertheless admired the way in which they functioned, particularly their expertise in collecting and increasing their revenues. The Dutch were reported to make 'places conquered or fortify'd, to pay the charge of their preservacion, as well as the first Cost of their Settlement...' .[109] The English factors were advised at regular intervals to imitate Dutch methods in order to 'make the English Nation, as formidable as the Dutch, or any other Europe Nation, are or ever were in India ...'.[110] They attributed the skill of the Dutch not only to the fact of their 'engrosment of spice' but also to their ability to make the 'Natives pay the charge of their fortified places ...'.[111] The factors on the coast tried to justify their position by saying that the Dutch raised revenue only in the places they conquered, and not from places like Pulicat and Batavia, but the Court of Directors at London refused to pay any attention to them. They agreed that the Dutch did not have 'sovereign authority [in Pulicat], nor the entire Customes', which was the reason for their war with

Golconda, but failed to see why Madras, with all the advantages gained by the original grant, and the freedom of trade there, could not increase its revenues. On the contrary, they said that Madras ought to do better than Pulicat, for the latter would never attract as many traders as Madras did, as this would affect the Dutch monopoly.

By the end of the seventeenth century, the English position had improved, and as the Court of Directors said, it was no longer possible for the Dutch to call them a 'parcel of meere trading merchants or pedlars . . .'.[112] Some amount of cooperation between the two Companies had begun from the 1680s, when, in addition to the East India Company, another group of merchants (called the Interlopers) had been granted a charter to trade by Charles II. The Interlopers were regarded as a greater threat, and so the English often asked the Dutch for help in keeping them out.

Towards the end of the century, problems flared up once again, but the English, at any rate, did not want to go to war, because it would 'be thought by the Vulgar but a Warr for Pepper'. They did realize, however, that a confrontation would have to come sooner or later, both for 'the dominion of the British as well as the Indian seas', for otherwise, the Dutch would have a total monopoly of all the spices. This would naturally give them all the economic benefits, and would also allow them to defray the expenses of a large navy in Europe.[113]

In the long run, Dutch methods themselves led to the Dutch losing their initial primacy. Dutch methods of finance and payment grew steadily more cumbersome, requiring, as they did, approval from Holland before anything could be done. In the case of the English, the promotion of private trade, and the increased dependence on the customs from trade as much as the trade itself, led to less bureaucratization, and consequently, easier and more direct links between London and India. From the 1690s, as the English Company managed to streamline its activities, the Dutch increasingly withdrew into the far south and Sri Lanka. This left the field clear for the English, for the French, though established at Pondicherri since the late 1690s, had too many problems at home in France to be able to offer any sustained threat until the eighteenth century.

The general decline in the trade of the Coromandel in the closing years of the seventeenth century and the beginning of the eighteenth century probably ended the Anglo-Dutch compettition. Suspicion continued, for in 1702, when there was a possibility of a war with France, it was said that the Dutch would not help the English, 'but underhand the Contrary…' .[114] In 1711, it was reported that the Dutch investments on the coast had been far lower than usual[115] and by 1713, the Dutch were trying to borrow money from the Armenian inhabitants of Madras, without any success.[116]

Incidentally, from the 1690s, in fact, Anglo-French rivalry was becoming more serious. Warnings were sent to English ships of the arrival of the French fleet in 1691, and English captains were advised to put into Dutch-controlled ports if necessary, to avoid the French.[117] In 1701, the Indian merchants at Fort St. David refused to enter into a contract with the English at the same prices as formerly, because the French had made such large investments that all prices had gone up.[118] A little later, it was discovered that many of the washers had left for Pondicherri, for the French paid higher rates than the English.[119]

Problems with the French escalated steadily, so much so, that in 1709, it was decided to send a 'black fellow… on each Vessell to go up to Madras with the … Compas. bales to own the goods as his in case of any disturbance from the French'.[120] As is well known, the final settlement of these problems was only after the Anglo-French wars of the Carnatic.

The seventeenth century was, in the south, a period of multiple political shifts. The entire debate of the eighteenth century, regarding continuity and change, or prosperity and decline, can equally well be applied to seventeenth-century south India. A century of paradoxes, it saw both, closer ties of the Indian economy with the world market, and the beginning of the process of decline. Much more than earlier, the Indian economy was tied into world market conditions, and so was susceptible to its fluctuations. For example, in the course of the seventeenth century, the English gradually began to change the kinds of textiles they bought, from the coarser varieties to the finer ones. Finer textiles required more of an initial investment or advance, which had to be made through the Indian merchants. But orders were placed on the basis of projections of the market two years later—so if, in the meantime, trends had changed, fresh orders would reflect the changed trends, and thus affect the weavers as well. When these fluctuations were added to increasingly chaotic political conditions at home, the weavers and merchants were forced to function within steadily narrowing limits, until finally, their only security lay within the bounds of the Company's trade. As pointed out earlier, in the process of ensuring its own position, and the trade of its employees, the Company gradually moved into the acquisition of political power. This process has, of course, been well documented for the eighteenth century, but the groundwork had been laid earlier.

Notes

1. M.N. Pearson, *Before Colonialism: Theories on Asian-European Relations, 1500–1750*, Delhi: Oxford University Press, 1988, quoting Niels Steensgaard, 'The Return Cargoes of the Carreira in the 16th and early 17th Centuries', in *Indo-Portuguese History: Old Issues, New Questions*, ed. T.R. de Souza, New Delhi, 1985, p. 22.
2. Om Prakash, 'The Portuguese and the Dutch in Asian Maritime trade: a Comparative Analysis', in *Merchants, Companies and Trade: Europe and*

Asia in the Early Modern Era, ed. Sushil Chaudhury and Michel Morineau, Cambridge: Cambridge University Press, 1999, pp. 175–88.

3. T. Wolseley Haig and K. Ahmed, eds., Khafi Khan's *Muntakhab-ul-Lubab*, 2 vols., vol. II, p. 367.
4. W. Foster, ed., *The English Factories in India* (henceforth *EFI*), Oxford: Clarendon Press, 1906–27, n.s., ed. C. Fawcett, 4 vols., 1642–5, p. 184.
5. Ibid., p. 45.
6. R. Sathianatha Aiyar, *History of the Nayaks of Madura*, Oxford: Oxford University Press, 1924, p. 127.
7. *EFI*, 1642–5, p. 116.
8. C.S. Srinivasachari, *History of Gingee and its Rulers*, Annamalai: Annamalai University Press, 1943, pp. 162–3.
9. *EFI*, 1642–5, p. 193.
10. V. Vriddhagirisan, *The Nayaks of Tanjore*, Annamalai: Annamalai University Press, 1942, p. 140.
11. S.N. Sen, ed., *The Indian Travels of Thévenot and Careri*, account of Thevenot, New Delhi: National Archives of India, 1949, p. 91.
12. *EFI*, 1651–4, p. 99; H.D. Love, ed., *Vestiges of Old Madras*, 3 vols., London, 1913 (henceforth *Vestiges*), vol. 1, p. 107.
13. *EFI*, 1655–60, p. 97.
14. Ibid., pp. 97–8.
15. V. Vriddhagirisan, op. cit., pp. 146–7.
16. R. Sathianatha Aiyar, op. cit., p. 165.
17. These and other details regarding Madanna are based on H.K. Sherwani, *History of the Qutb Shahi Dynasty*, Delhi: Munshiram Manoharlal, 1974, and Y.H. Khan, ed., *Farmans and Sanads of the Deccan Sultans*, Hyderabad, 1963.
18. *Vestiges*, vol. I, section on chief merchants at Madras.
19. J.F. Richards, *Mughal Administration in Golconda*, Delhi: Oxford University Press, 1975.
20. G.S. Sardesai, *New History of the Marathas*, 3 vols., Bombay, revd. edn, 1956, vol. I, pp. 215–25.
21. Jadunath Sarkar, *History of Aurangzeb*, 5 vols., Calcutta: M.C. Sarkar and Sons, 1912–30, vol. IV, p. 335.
22. He did not stick to the latter part of the agreement. Instead, in addition to the already existing kingdom of Thanjavur, he also established Maratha strongholds at Jinji and Vellore.
23. Records of Fort St. George, *Diary and Consultation Books* (henceforth RFSG, *Diary*), 9 May 1677.
24. Ibid., 14 May 1677.
25. Ibid., 18 June 1677.
26. Ibid., 3 October 1677.
27. Ibid., 8 April 1678.
28. Ibid., 21 August 1678.
29. Jadunath Sarkar, op. cit., vol. IV, p. 345.
30. Jadunath Sarkar, tr. and ed., *Saqi Musta'id Khan's Ma'asir-i-Alamgiri* (henceforth Sarkar, tr. and ed., *Ma'asir*), Calcutta, 1947, p. 164.

31. Ibid., p. 174.
32. Ibid., p. 177. Trenches were ordered to be dug from 7 February 1687.
33. Ibid.
34. RFSG, *Diary*, 21 November 1687.
35. Ibid., 28 November 1687.
36. Ibid., 14 November 1687.
37. Ibid., 12 December 1687 and 16 January 1688; J.F. Richards, *Mughal Administration in Golconda*, op. cit., chaps. V and VI.
38. Sarkar, tr. and ed., *Ma'asir*, op. cit., p. 202.
39. RFSG, *Diary*, 26 December 1687.
40. Ibid., 5 February 1696.
41. Sarkar, tr. and ed., *Ma'asir*, op. cit., p. 238.
42. RFSG, *Diary*, 20 March 1674.
43. RFSG, *Despatches from England, Letter to Fort St. George*, 2 July 1684.
44. Ibid., *Letter to Fort St. George*, 12 August 1685.
45. RFSG, *Diary*, 1 August 1687.
46. RFSG, *Despatches from England, Letter to Fort St. George*, 1698/99.
47. *EFI*, 1624–9, p 281.
48. Ibid., 1622–3, p. 46.
49. Ibid., 1618–21, p. 265.
50. Ibid., 1622–3, p. 46.
51. Ibid., 1624–9, p. 282.
52. Ibid., pp. 317–18.
53. *Vestiges*, vol. I, p. 15.
54. *EFI*, 1655–60, p. 137.
55. RFSG, *Diary*, 9 August 1678.
56. Ibid., 11 February 1679.
57. R.C. Temple, ed., *The Diaries of Streynsham Master, 1675–1680, and Other Contemporary Papers Relating Thereto*, in 2 vols., vol. I, London, 1911, p. 75.
58. RFSG, *Diary*, 6 April 1681.
59. Ibid., 6 January 1681.
60. RFSG, *Despatches from England*, 2 July 1684.
61. Ibid.
62. RFSG, *Diary*, 1 May 1690.
63. W.H. Moreland, *From Akbar to Aurangzeb: A Study in Indian Economic History*, London, 1923; Delhi: Munshiram Manoharlal, rpt, 1972, p. 221.
64. Ibid.
65. M.L. Dames, tr. and ed., *The Book of Duarte Barbosa*, 2 vols., London: Hakluyt Society, 1918, vol. II, p. 77.
66. *EFI*, 1622–3, pp. 51–2.
67. Ibid., p. 337.
68. H. Heras, *Studies in the Aravidu Dynasty of Vijayanagar*, Madras: G. Paul & Co., 1927, p. 443.
69. Ibid., p. 453.
70. This apparently refers to the Tuticorin Bay, which was under the control of the Nayak of Madurai.

71. S. Arasaratnam, 'The Dutch East India Company and the Kingdom of Madura, 1650–1700', *Tamil Culture*, 1963, pp. 47–74.
72. RFSG, *Diary*, 16 February 1681.
73. Ibid., 20 March 1674.
74. *EFI*, 1634–6, p. 14.
75. *Vestiges*, vol. I, p. 17; *EFI*, 1637–43, pp. 156–8.
76. Ibid., p. 20.
77. RFSG, *Diary*, 15 August 1690.
78. S.N. Sen, ed., *The Indian Travels of Thévenot and Careri*, op. cit., p. 111.
79. Lotika Varadarajan, tr. and ed., *India of the 17th Century: Memoirs of Francois Martin*, vol. I, pt. I, Delhi: Manohar, 1981, p. 120 and *passim*.
80. *Annual Report on South Indian Epigraphy* (henceforth *ARSIE*), *ARSIE* copper plate no. 11 of 1935–6.
81. RFSG, *Letters to Fort St. George*, 9 January 1682.
82. Ibid., 12 January 1682.
83. RFSG, *Despatches from England, Letter to Fort St. George*, 22 March 1687.
84. J.F. Richards, 'European City-States on the Coromandel Coast', in *Studies in the Foreign Relations of India: Prof. H.K. Sherwani Felicitation Volume*, ed. P.M. Joshi and M.A. Nayeem, Hyderabad, 1975, pp. 508–21.
85. RFSG, *Diary*, 1690.
86. Ibid., 16 February 1691.
87. RFSG, *Fort St. David Consultations*, 13 January 1698.
88. Ibid., 24 January 1698.
89. Ibid., 29 April 1698.
90. Ibid., 8 June 1698.
91. Ibid., 1 August 1701.
92. RFSG, *Diary*, 1701
93. Ibid., 29 January 1702.
94. RFSG, *Fort St. David Consultations*, 10 February 1702.
95. RFSG, *Diary*, 7 February 1702.
96. Ibid., 11 February 1702.
97. J.F. Richards, 'The Imperial Crisis in the Deccan', *Journal of Asian Studies*, vol. 35, no. 2, February 1976, pp. 237–56.
98. RFSG, *Fort St. David Consultations*, 7 May 1698.
99. *Vestiges*, vol. I, p. 50.
100. C.S. Srinivasachari, *History of Gingee and its Rulers, passim.*
101. Sanjay Subrahmanyam, *The Portuguese Empire in Asia, 1500–1700: A Political and Economic History*, London and New York: Longman, 1993; and Sanjay Subrahmanyam, *Improvising Empire Portuguese Trade and Settlement in the Bay of Bengal, 1500–1700*, Delhi: Oxford University Press, 1990.
102. French trade became an important factor only towards the end of the seventeenth century. The Danes, the only other Europeans on the coast, had a single factory, Tranquebar, and a virtually negligible presence.
103. H. Furber, *Rival Empires of Trade in the Orient, 1600–1800*, Minneapolis: University of Minnesota Press, 1976, p. 268.
104. Quoted in N. Steensgard, *The Asian Trade Revolution of the 17th Century:*

The East India Companies and the Decline of the Caravan Trade, Chicago: University of Chicago Press, 1974, p. 407.

105. As the Malabar, Madagascar and other pirates discovered later in the century.
106. RFSG, *Despatches to England, Letter from Pitt to London*, 19 February 1702.
107. RFSG, *Despatches from England, Letter to Fort St. George*, 8 January 1674.
108. Ibid., 1683.
109. Ibid., *Letter to Fort St. George*, 20 July 1683.
110. Ibid., 26 August 1685.
111. Ibid., 14 January 1685.
112. Ibid., 9 June 1686.
113. Ibid., 3 August 1686.
114. RFSG, *Despatches to England, Letter from Pitt to London*, 19 February 1702.
115. Ibid., 4 September 1711.
116. Ibid., 11 January 1713.
117. RFSG, *Diary*, 2 January 1691.
118. RFSG, *Fort St. David Consultations*, 2 August 1701.
119. Ibid., 14 December 1702.
120. Ibid., 3 March 1709.

CHAPTER 3

'Shoes, Ships and Sealing Wax': Chief Merchants and Others

TRADE, AS HAS been shown earlier in this study, was long-established, and had its own rhythms, dictated no doubt by the seasonal variations of winds and tides, but also governed by the laws of supply and demand. Several questions arise: Who were the traders? What was their precise role in economic, social and/or political terms? In fact, *did* they have a political role? And if so, how did they combine political and economic roles, if such a combination were either possible or necessary? It is easy enough to talk in general terms about the value (or otherwise) of trade and traders, to society and the state, but one problem that we face for the pre-modern world is a dearth of names of individuals, especially on the east coast, who can be clearly identified.

The main trading community in south India was (and continues to be) the Chettis. The word itself is believed to be a corruption of *sethi* or *setti* which was apparently a more or less generic term for merchant, along with the more formal *vanijya*. In the south the majority of the population was involved in at least some amount of mercantile activity. The Chettis, however, appear to have been the one group that was involved only in commercial enterprises. Such enterprises may and often did include association with local or urban administrative bodies but, occupationally, they remained merchants. Among them, we find many subdivisions: for instance, the Beri Chetti (apparently Telugu merchants) and the Komati Chetti (presumably Tamil merchants: the English records refer to this group as 'Committees'). Late in the nineteenth century, the Komatis were described by E. Thurston as the 'great trading Caste of the Madras Presidency',[1] many of whom were involved in the cloth trade. Early in the twentieth century, a specific group of Chettis, the Nattukottai Chettis, who, according to their own traditions are descended from the guild of the 500, were said to be the brokers, moneylenders and wholesale merchants for all south India.[2] However, in the seventeenth century, no such specific subdivision seems to have existed, for considering that they seem to have combined the important functions of brokerage and moneylending, the

European records would certainly have mentioned the existence of such a group.

The Chettis too seem to have been part of that unique vertical division in south India of the left-hand and right-hand castes, the *idangai-valangai* (see Appendix I). It has been suggested that this marks the division between the agricultural/artisanal groups and the industrial/mercantile groups. In the Chola period, this may have referred to military divisions,[3] but later, by the time of Vijayanagar, the *idangai-valangai* comprised different professional castes, who were involved in intense social conflict. However, Buchanan lists merchants and weavers in both groups;[4] for example, he has 'Bheri Chetti' (Beri Chetti) in the left hand, and the 'Baniji-garu' (clearly derived from the older *vanijya*, and here also referring to Telugu merchants, as the use of the word 'garu' implies) as being members of the right. Interestingly, he includes in his lists the Gujaratis who lived in the south, implying that this caste division could be stretched to include merchants from other parts of India as well. However, it should be remembered that his was a much later description, and actually belongs to a time when this division was on the decline.

Clashes between the two were frequent even in the seventeenth and early eighteenth centuries, as, for example, in Madras in 1652 and 1707,[5] and apparently at Pulicat also.[6] The factors at Fort St. George reported to the Court of Directors in 1652 that 'the country round about, as well as this and all other towns in this Kingdome, are divided into Two Generall Casts, namely the Belgewarres [Balija-varu] and the Bereewarres [Beri-varu], who for many hundred years together have ever had a Quarell one with the other who Should be the more honourable Cast and have Presidency [precedence] of the other'[7]. At this time, the Madras Council under the Presidentship of Aaron Baker drew up a detailed list of which streets were earmarked for which castes and further stated that 'Sheshadree Chittee, as madiator to each Cast, his servants nor the Companys servants and Painters cannot pass these streets'.[8]

The south did not seem to have any organization of merchants similar to the Banjaras of the north, for long-distance internal trade. In earlier times, the guilds were probably involved in such operations. However, no information is available as to the number of animals and/or carts kept by these merchants, whether there were specific routes allotted to different groups of merchants, how much tax was paid on each animal or cart, or how much was usually carried by each group of merchants—with the result that no estimate can be made of the volume of trade.

Inscriptions do mention the *peruvali* or 'big roads'[9] which refer to well-used trade routes, as well as to *milagu taragam*, which is taken to mean the route by which pepper was transported from the west to the east coast. Travel accounts refer to routes that were regularly used between Vijayanagar and Goa and Bankapur and from Vijayanagar through Kanchipuram to Mailapur, now a suburb of Chennai, but an important trading station in earlier times.

Moreover, we have no information on how the trade was financed. Barbosa remarked on the wealth of the Chettis at Malacca, and said that they measured their wealth only by '*bahar* of gold'.[10] While this might be an exaggeration, it is also probably a good indication of the wealth of the Indian merchant community. Both in the seventeenth century and earlier, bullion was an important import into India; there are frequent references in Portuguese and other European accounts of 'gold for the coast of Coromandel'.[11] This gold could be either as coin or as ingots to be coined, but again, there is no information about the methods of minting coins or of money-changing, or even of commission for such activities. In the seventeenth century, when the English had acquired mint facilities at Chennai, though they had handed over the charge of the mint to the Komati Chettis, they made sure that they supervised the mint. Maratha records of the eighteenth century provide some details about the establishment of mints, their supervisions, and both the existence and possibilities of fraud, but such details are not available for the earlier centuries. We know still less about the cost of transport, internal or external, the extent to which it affected prices, or if and when goods were freighted, the charges for such freight, or even the insurance (if it existed) on such transportation.

Nevertheless, it may be possible to divide merchants into various categories, based on the nature of commercial activity in which they were involved. Such categories were by no means mutually exclusive; on the contrary, many overlapped, and often a single merchant was involved in a wide range of activities. The categories seem to be found in the guilds also, which talk of *nanadesi, paradesi*, and *svadesi* merchants. Translations of the terms are varied, but on the whole, it appears that the first group comprised merchants who lived in India, and traded both within India and to other countries. The second group probably comprised non-Indians involved in Indian trade, or merchants involved only in export trade, while the third group probably consisted of merchants involved exclusively in internal trade.

In the seventeenth century, the categories of merchants included, first, shipowners, involved in long-distance and in country trade (i.e. the port-to-port trade of the coast). The scale of operations could vary, from people like Mir Jumla who was reported to own 10 ships, to others who had perhaps one ship. Surat records refer to the families of Virji Vora and Abdul Ghafur owning 40 ships. However, we have scant information about the size of these ships. In the 1630s, one of Mir Jumla's ships was reported to be of 500 tons burden, while earlier, in 1622, one ship on the Gujarat-Red Sea route was reported to be of 450 tons, which would seem to indicate that such sizes were fairly normal. Travel accounts of the late sixteenth and early seventeenth century talk of ships of Indian merchants of 600 tons or more. Later records of the west coast refer to *galivats* plying along the coast, and used by Kanhoji Angré early in the eighteenth century. These ships were supposed to be light and easily manoeuvrable, and ideal for the country trade. Similar statements are to be found about the catamarans of the east coast. The larger ships definitely carried freight, so that even merchants who did not own ships were involved in export trade. Members of the royal family, especially the Mughals, were also participants in this freight trade. These, perhaps, correspond to the *nanadesis* of the earlier period. However, like other details we have no information about freight charges. Some figures for marine freight are available for the west coast, but none for the east coast, until we come to the English factory records and the information that they supply on freight charges on Company ships.

Another category of merchants were those dealing in the commodities of import and export. They usually had extensive links in the hinterland, which enabled them to distribute the imported goods as well as supply those required for export. It is possible that the Chief Merchants of the East India Companies, about whom we get a great deal of information, belonged to this category. In addition to these, were merchants who were involved in money-changing or moneylending activities—the *sarrafs* of the north being a prime example.

Outside India, there is no doubt that Indian and Asian merchants were extremely active. William Methwold, writing in the early seventeenth century, declared that the Indians 'build great ships ... some of them not lesse than 600 tunnes. ... With these their ships they traffique ordinarily to Mocha in the Red Sea, to Achyne upon Sumatra, to Arrecan, Pegu, and Tenassery on the other side of the Gulfe, and to many ports alongst their owne coasts, as farr as Zeloan [Sri Lanka] and the Cape Comoryne.'[12] At Malacca, the presence of the Bengal, Masulipattinam and Pegu merchants hindered the English Company's purchases.[13] As early as 1620, the English factors at Masulipattinam had declared that the 'welth and welfare of the kingdome of Gulcondah doth consist in itts inland manyfactures, which findes most or all his vent by sea transporte ... '.[14] Later in the century, when English trade had been affected by the exigencies of the wars that had until then been taking place, they reported that, though their trade was 'much decayed within this fewe yeares, ... the Moores doe trade more than they ever did'.[15] In the 1670s, Abbé Carré reported meeting Indian merchants at Genoa.[16]

While it is possible to distinguish varieties of commercial activities, merchants with a larger reach often combined all of them. In other words, they were involved in export and import, as well as in moneylending activities. However, in the course of the seventeenth century, the scale of operations of the Indian merchants began to decrease. Increasingly, they limited themselves to one category of operations, that of the middleman/broker (*dubash*) involved in supplying the articles required by the Europeans. Those appointed as Chief Merchants were important, but in that capacity, more than as independent traders.

The role of the broker/middleman was an extremely important one. In Gujarat, many who worked with the Europeans in this capacity were important merchants in their own right—men like Virji Vora, for instance, who supplied the Europeans with the goods they needed, but also competed with them. From the very beginning, the Europeans had seen the need for a *dubash*, who would be able to purchase the goods required by them. Such brokers, on the west coast, could be either independent merchants engaged on a percentage commission, or, more rarely, employees of the Factory at Surat. The south, however, does not show merchants of like stature. As mentioned earlier, the names that we do find are of the Chief Merchants. Brokers are mentioned late in the seventeenth century, in connection with the trade in precious stones, as having leased the office from the Company.[17] The brokerage fee was clearly stated, as also was the amount to be paid to the Company.

However, brokers held a far more important role in supplying textiles. In south India, weavers tended to be widely scattered in the interior, and according to the Europeans, very mobile—all they needed was trees under which to set up their looms. This meant, on the one hand, that more brokers were needed to go into the country to supervise or collect the goods that had been commissioned; and on the other, that regular attempts were also being made to get the weavers to settle in the vicinity of the forts. As the weavers were generally too poor to purchase any of the material they required, the system of advances was absolutely necessary. The factors pointed out that the weavers never undertook any work without it, and said that it had been 'customary and of course to deliver money aforehand to the Merchants for the more timely accomplishing of their investments'.[18]

It was calculated that 'to provide hundred thousand pagodas worth of Callicoes, he must be fain to give out for above half so much more to allow for disappointments …'.[19] Early in the eighteenth century, the factors at Madras noted that an advance of 300 pagodas was given to the painters to paint 300 pieces of blue cloth, named *muris* in the records.[20] The merchants therefore acted as contractors for the provision of cotton cloth (as well as agents for the sale of goods brought out from Europe). Money to be advanced to the weavers was given to the merchants, who were then responsible for delivering the finished goods; and the advances were also in the form of a contract with the weaver, ensuring that he would supply the required quantity. London sent lists of the Company's requirements to the factories, after which the factors issued musters to their brokers, together with the maximum price to be paid. These musters were stamped with the

Company's seal, and then delivered to the weavers along with the advances. Thereafter, the finished cloth was delivered to the Company's warehouses, where it was compared with the original muster. It was generally presumed that the original and the finished product did not match, and so, even before sorting, payment was made on the basis of the cloth being of the 'lowest sort'. After sorting, the final payment was made. Interestingly, there exist frequent complaints about the strictness of the sorting.

Differences existed in the methods of commissioning various kinds of cloth. In 1678, the Masulipattinam factors reported that the finer varieties were 'provided by persons of as plentiful Estates as reputation and experience, and therefore need no further anticipation of moneys for carrying on the work [except what was customary], that is one moyety [half payment] upon contract'.[21] The merchants involved in providing the coarser varieties were usually poorer, and therefore needed larger advances.

As has been mentioned earlier, the guilds dominated much of the commercial scene until about the thirteenth century, after which we begin to get a few names of individual merchants. Numerous merchants began to be increasingly involved with the *nagarams*, but nevertheless continued with their trading activities. The nature of the links between merchants and the administrative networks needs to be studied in more depth for these centuries. But the fact is that by the time we come to the seventeenth century, there exist more instances of a combination of roles of merchant and administrator. Such roles are particularly visible in Golconda and Vijayanagar in the first half of the seventeenth century.

In this connection, it can be pointed out that the two dominant figures of the first half of the seventeenth century were Malaya Chetti and Mir Jumla. Malaya and his extended family were active in both trade and politics of the Coromandel Coast until almost 1659. Mir Jumla, as is well known, very comfortably combined trading and political activities within the Golconda kingdom.

Malaya Chetti, also referred to as Astrappa or Achyutappa Chetti, was one of the most important merchants of the early seventeenth century. He was a major shipowner and trader, whose ships were sent from the two main bases of operation: Pulicat and Devanamapattinam, as well as from other ports of the Coromandel to Arakan, Pegu, Tenasserim, Kedah, Aceh and Sri Lanka.[22] Members of Malaya's family were active in both commercial and political ventures in different parts of the Coromandel for much of the first half of the seventeenth century. And, Malaya himself became chief broker of the Dutch at Pulicat. It is possible to surmise that the Dutch tried to settle in Devanamapattinam because of Malaya's connections there, and later established themselves at Pulicat for the same reason. In 1632, Malaya contracted with the Dutch to supply textiles worth 23,000 pagodas.[23] Until his death, he, and after his death, his brother Chinanna supplied the

Company with varieties of cloth, and shipped larger amounts on their own account.[24]

Malaya was, in addition to being a trader, a tax farmer. In 1633, he got the farm of Pulicat's revenues on the payment of 33,000 pagodas,[25] and also collected the customs on imports and exports for some years. Apparently, he defrauded the Dutch Company and the merchants in his capacity as collector of customs duties—something that became a bone of contention later, when the Dutch began to deduct 1,000 pagodas annually from the rent of Pulicat.[26] He also took the farm for Devanamapattinam, where, too, the Dutch had a factory, thus becoming their landlord at both places. In addition, he took the lease of the Danish fort in Tranquebar: Dutch attempts to get a sublease of the fort from him were foiled by the Nayak of Thanjavur.[27]

Malaya's brother Chinanna[28] was an important merchant and tax farmer in his own right. Even more active in court politics than his brother, particularly at the court of Krishnappa Nayak of Jinji, in the 1630s, he led an armed force in favour of Jinji's contender to the throne. In 1636–7, he acted as the Nayak's emissary in talks with the Nayaks of Madurai and Thanjavur.[29] However, Chinanna and the Nayak had a falling out in 1638, at which time Chinanna's fort in Devanamapattinam was destroyed by the Nayak.[30] In a fight between Chinanna, his nephew Koneri Chetti and a Jinji noble Tupaki Krishnappa Nayak (who commanded Sriranga's troops and later became Mir Jumla's lieutenant), Chinanna was defeated, and moved to Pulicat, to become the Dutch chief broker in place of his brother Malaya. The differences between Chinanna and the Nayak were later resolved, and Chinanna re-established himself in Devanamapattinam—without, however, giving up his activities as chief broker.

Chinanna's political activities seem to have continued even after his shift to Pulicat, with the only difference that these activities now tended to centre on Chandragiri, the capital of the truncated Vijayanagar Empire, and Sriranga, the last Vijayanagar king. He offered his services to the king in 1643, with Dutch artillery and support. The English saw the latter as an attempt by the Dutch to gain a monopoly over Coromandel trade, for they wrote that the Dutch 'have bine a projecting and now they have wrought it that Mollay, their merchant, is like to bee as powerfull with this king as the Serkayle [*Sar-i-Khail*, i.e. Mir Jumla] is att Gulcondah; and, to ingratiate him thoroughly into his favour, they have assisted Mollay with men and gunns for the subdueing of castles … for the king …'.[31] The Dutch later withdrew support to the merchant, perhaps because they were afraid of losing control over their broker, and members of Chinanna's family still at Pulicat were imprisoned. Chinanna retaliated by besieging Pulicat, and seizing one of the Company's merchants at Tiruvattur. Subsequently, a Dutch force sent out from Pulicat was defeated, and the English, rather gleefully, reported that the great difference betwixt the Dutch and Mollay . . . is now fallen into open warrs. . . . Soe that it is come to such a pass through Molays meanes, who is in such favour with the King that he ruleth both King and Contry, and hath prevaled soe farr with the King to send his Mandates to all his Governours throughout his kingdome to seaze upon all the goods which is in any Jentue Merchants hands belonging unto the Dutch, and whosoever shall be found to deny any of their goods, that party to be seazed upon and all his estate forfeited to the King. . . .[32]

The English certainly reaped benefits, for they accepted the confiscated Dutch goods.[33] The Dutch were saved only by the invasion of Golconda, at which time Chinanna was ordered to the defence of Udayagiri, which was besieged by Mir Jumla. Chinanna was forced to surrender, and returned to Pulicat.

Around 1657, Chinanna shifted his base of operations to the Thanjavur kingdom, and leased the revenues of Nagapattinam for about 40,000 pagodas per year.[34] He continued to maintain his present position, i.e. of revenue farmer even after the expansion of Bijapur. The only difference was that he now leased the ports of Devanamapattinam and Alambaram from the Bijapur commander rather than the Thanjavur Nayak.[35] After the Dutch captured Nagapattinam from the Portuguese, Chinanna was apparently instrumental in getting them a grant from the then Nayak of Thanjavur, Vijayaraghava. The grant began by saying that 'Chinnanna Setti, had earnestly submitted to us by means of petitions that your company was very desirous of carrying on trade operations in the port of Nagapatnam. . . . Therefore, as desired by him, you are permitted to come to Nagapatnam to carry on trade.'[36]

Another outstanding personality of the first half of the seventeenth century is Mir Jumla. Here again, it must be stressed that Mir Jumla, far from being an exception, fit perfectly into the established mode of Persian emigrants into the Deccan who transcended the so-called merchant/politics divide. To go a little further back, the first half of the fifteenth century had seen extensive commercial contacts between the western Deccan and the Persian Gulf ports, where the Kazaruni merchants (belonging to the area near Shiraz) were important;[37] later in the same century we have Mahmud Gawan Gilani, *wazir* of the Bahmani kingdom, who belonged to a family with widerspread mercantile links.[38]

Mir Muhammad Said Ardestani arrived in the Deccan in the retinue of a horse-trader, then went on to farm a diamond mine, proceeded to branch out into trade across the Bay of Bengal, and then, in succession, was the *sardaftardar* in Hyderabad, *havaldar* in the Nizamapattinam region, and finally, Mir Jumla of the Golconda Sultanate.[39] His influence in the empire was such that he was second in command to the Sultan himself; while the scope of his mercantile activities in no way decreased. On the contrary, he was believed to have branched out into moneylending also. He loaned money to the English at Masulipattinam in 1642–3, and again at Madras in 1646–7.[40] Repayment of such loans was made according to Mir Jumla's needs, whether political or mercantile, for in one instance, it took the form of a brass gun.[41] His clout was such that in 1651, the English at Fort St. George reported that the 'whole kingdom of Gulcondah is governed by him . . .'. They went on to say that he brought in, annually, revenues to the tune of 'twentye hundred thousand pagodas', and that he had,

> of his proper owne four thousand horse, three hundred elephants, four or five hundred cammels, and ten thousand oxen, which transporteth his goods up into severall countrys, as Gulcondah, Vizapore and into dyvers parts of the Great Moguls country. . . . Concerning forran navigation, he hath trade to Pegue, Tenasaree, Acheen, Rackan, Persia, Bengalla, Moka, Peruk, Moldeevaes, and Macassar. He hath tenn vessels of his owne, and intends to augment them, making much preparation for building of more.[42]

Later in the same year, Mir Jumla also tried to get a monopoly of cloth—the English reported that:

> not . . . a piece [was] to bee sold but by his owne ministers, who are to engross all from the weavers and have order to rate them at 20% profitt to whomsoever will buy, or keepe them in his warehouses . . .; and this course he is resolved to continue, untill hee can bring a monopoly upon all imported goods.[43]

Later, even after he defected to the Mughals, he kept up his trading activities through his agents, who operated in 'Pallacatt, Metchlepatam, etc. places of Cuttubshawes [Qutb Shah's] dominion, by vertue of the Moghors power'.[44]

Malaya, Chinanna and Mir Jumla are not solitary examples of their kind. The Khan-i-Khanan of Bijapur, who was also the governor of those areas of Karnataka conquered by Bijapur, was reported to own ships which he used in extensive overseas trade, while also appointing merchants to trade on his behalf.[45] Other names include in Golconda, Muhammad Taqi, who was a governor and merchant of Masulipattinam (in which capacity he put numerous obstacles in the way of the English trade), Mir Kamaluddin, and Mir Muhammad Murad. Frequent references are found in both Dutch and English records to the participation of Mir Jumla and Mir Kamaluddin in the Red Sea trade. The Dutch discovered that the latter had sent cargoes of cloth and sapan wood to Persia, that he had purchased from the Dutch. The Dutch were unable to do anything about it.[46] Further south, members of Malaya's family—Chinanna, Sesadri, Koneri and Lakshmana, to name a few—continued to be important.

Can these two figures then be called portfolio-capitalists? The theory of portfolio-capitalism argues that, in the pre-modern Indian world, there began to emerge a class that could tread the two worlds of politics and trade with remarkable ease. The core of this theory is the understanding that though spheres of activity may have been different and distinct, yet, there was no reason why they should stay separate. In certain crucial instances, they could and did overlap, often to an individual's benefit. Contrary to the perceived advantages to those who maintained separate and distinct identities, there were individuals who combined both the roles, and used each to bolster the other. Such individuals are termed 'portfolio' and 'capitalist' because they did, at least to some extent, combine the two roles. Many were members of the administration, and held 'portfolios' in some kingdom. Moreover, as influential members of the nobility, they had access to power, and probably to information. While this position ensured status, it may not necessarily have meant a great deal of income, for the income of the state had to be divided among innumerable people. For additional personal income, therefore, there had to be a sphere of activity that was not part of the official position. Those who were capable thus took to different aspects of commercial activity—in effect becoming early merchant 'capitalists'. In this capacity, they could advance money on interest, get involved in various ventures of export and import, or build ships to either directly engage in long distance overseas ventures, or rent out space on these ships for freight. Within the ambit of such activities, they could then use their political position to gain advantages that would have been denied to the average merchant.

In many ways then, the nomenclature of a 'portfolio-capitalists' to Malaya Chetti and Mir Jumla fits, perhaps more so for the latter than the former. Both were important in their respective administrative systems—given the fact that Golconda was, in the early seventeenth century a much larger and more important kingdom than Vijayanagar, the scale of Mir Jumla's activities was necessarily much larger. Malaya Chetti in his role as commander of the Vijayanagar army besieged Pulicat, and threatened considerable damage to Dutch trade there. Obviously, he had the capacity to do so. He was the broker to the Dutch company, and interestingly did not stop supplying goods to the company, but used his political position to ensure that the Dutch acceded to his terms. As pointed out earlier, he and his family were influential all along the coast, and used this influence at the local courts very effectively.

Mir Jumla provides an even better illustration of the theory. The scale of his operations—as merchant, moneylender, and commander-in-chief of the Golconda army has already been described. He did take passes from the European companies—a system that was now sufficiently well-established to be taken for granted—but the records seem to imply that these passes were taken as though by right, that he held out the threat of damaging the companies' trade if he were not given the passes. In one instance, the Dutch complained that he had taken their pass, and had sailed his ships to Sri Lanka, where they were then engaged in war against the Portuguese, and sold all the goods on board to the Portuguese. The Dutch were unable to do anything to stop him.

This, then, was the position that prevailed in the first half of the century. However, farther south, it is noticeable that, with the final collapse of the Vijayanagar Empire, there are no longer many instances of merchants being involved in politics. From now onwards, the shift to the forts begins to take place.

From the inception of the English settlement at Fort St. George, numerous merchants had been associated with it. The first Chief Merchant was Sesadri Chetti, usually referred to as 'our Merchant Sesadra [*sic*] Nague'. As mentioned earlier, he was a member of Malaya's family, and probably arrived at Madras along with Koneri Chetti shortly after 1640. Like his famed relative, Sesadri, too, was involved in local politics, for the English reported that Malaya (actually Chinanna) was supporting Sesadri in his efforts to become the 'sole Marchant in the King's Dominions'.[47] He was stated to be a trustworthy merchant, 'alwaies honestly clearing his Accompts, furnishing with good commodityes, and advancing the sale of our Europe goods, especially Corall. . .'.[48] However, he later lost the Company's favour to two Brahman brothers, Venkata and Kanappa. The latter had begun as *adigar* (headman) of Madras, but had risen to become Chief Merchant. Perhaps in an attempt to regain his position, Sesadri incited the first of the right-hand/left-hand caste disputes in Madras in 1652. Still later (around 1651), he was reported to owe the Company 'a greate summe of money'.[49]

Around 1662, Beri Timanna, 'the only person experienced and to be trusted'[50] (by the English) was appointed as the Company's Chief Merchant. His entire career came to be centred on Madras and the English Company. The factors said (in 1680) that there was a need for a *dubash* 'to find out good and able Merchants for improving the sale of our Europe goods...; which formerlye was Tymonas Imployment...'[51] Timanna began as a *dubash* and was apparently involved in the private trade of a Company factor (Greenhill). He later went on to become a toll collector. Timanna and his partner Rudriga were accused of taking 300 pagodas on goods taken out of, or brought into, the factory. They were imprisoned, and made to pay 1,500 pagodas to the Company.[52] However, the office did allow him to build up his personal fortune, and eventually become the Company's Chief Merchant. Unlike Sesadri, he did not belong to any of the established mercantile classes, nor did he have any influential contacts outside Madras. As a 'migrant with no identifiable associations with the region outside Madras, a member of a caste of relatively low status who had reached financial success and high ascribed status in the Company's service, Timanna far more than Sesadra [*sic*] identified himself with the Company and the enclave it dominated'.[53] It was as the Company's merchant that he managed to acquire certain privileges which were later inherited by subsequent Chief Merchants. These included the right of paying only half the customs 'upon all manner of goods that he should Import or Export at this towne by Sea or Land, whether the said goods be brought in for the Honble: Companies Accott: or brought in or carried out for the Accott: of himself singly or in partnership…'.[54] This concession was acquired as a result of a *qaul* from Neknam Khan. Timanna's partner as chief merchant was Kasi Viranna (or Hasan Khan), and after the former's death in 1669, Viranna continued as the Chief Merchant.

Kasi Viranna dominated the Madras scene until his death in 1680. Though involved in the Company's trade, he was also a merchant in his own right. Besides, Viranna also took up a few revenue farms of Armagon, Kottapattinam and San Thomé.[55] The merchant was comfortable dealing with both the Dutch and the French: Abbé Carré, a French priest at Madras, reported that, during the siege of the French in San Thomé by the Golconda troops, Viranna sent his men at night with information and supplies.[56] Earlier, complaints had been made to the Governor (at this time Foxcroft) against Timanna and Viranna, linking them with the private trade of an earlier Governor, Sir Edward Winter. It was alleged that contracts had been made at grossly inflated rates, while the amounts paid to the weavers were the normal ones. The difference was divided among the three. It was decided to imprison Timanna and Viranna, and further, that they 'should never be settled in the Choutry and Goverment of the Towne againe, or have the sole management of all buying and selling with the Company as before…'.[57] However, this resolve did not last for any great length of time, and before very long, Timanna and Viranna had regained the Company's favour, and were back in Madras, stronger than before.

By 1672, Viranna was apparently in a better position, for in that year, the factors at Fort St. George reported that Viranna and 'the heirs of Timonah' provided '3/4 of the … stock, Vizt. Pagodas 60 million'.[58] Four years later, in 1676, Viranna was accused of being a partner in the private trade of yet another Fort St. George Governor, Sir William Langhorne. With Viranna's help and active connivance, Langhorne reportedly received 20,000 pagodas annually. Viranna indignantly denied all charges, saying that all his dealings with the English were those of 'a free merchant, and no Servant of theirs …'. He added that it was 'not of late only that [he began] to trade with [the Company]' and his dealings had not been 'in private, but openly and publickly'.[59]

On the contrary, the Company still owed him 9,000 pagodas, which they had not repaid for 13 years.[60] In connection with this, Viranna wrote to the Court of Directors, claiming that the Company owed him 9,175 pagodas. The directors refused to accept any such liability; on the contrary, maintaining that Viranna and Timanna had defrauded them to the tune of nearly 2,00,000 pagodas. Furthermore, no mention of any debt had been made until 1669, and then too by Viranna alone, and not by his partners in the stock.[61] Nevertheless, that he was involved in at least some trade, either on his own account, or in conjunction with certain Company officials, is clear from the fact that, two years after these allegations and counter-allegations, in 1679, a parcel containing 'diamonds, bezoar and musk' was received at London. The value of this was £1,172 9s. 6d.; and Sambrooke, the person to whom this parcel was sent, had also borrowed another £126 from Viranna. It was decided that Sambrooke was to pay the full sum in London and bills of exchange for this sum were to be drawn on Fort St. George, payable to Viranna.[62]

The Court of Directors at London objected to the virtual monopoly that Viranna had over the Company's trade in Fort St. George. Desirous of increasing competition among Indian merchants, so as to get the best possible deal for the Company, they refused to believe that only one man was trustworthy enough to get the Company's contracts. If his presence was an advantage to Madras trade, then it was because the factors allowed him to 'grow and Remayne Master of that trade and therefore it is More then tyme to provide against the consequences of this Mischief Least ye continuance put it beyond remedy ...'.[63] Therefore, the factors were instructed to establish good relations with the governors of the cloth producing areas, so that Viranna could conduct business only as an employee of the Company.[64]

The Court of Directors' concern grew because of the time lapse between sending out the lists of supplies and actually getting the supplies—a gap of two years. The lists were drawn up on the basis of the market as it then existed, and tastes could (and did) change in two years. What made it worse was the fact that the cargo sent out from England consisted mainly of bullion. For instance, in 1675, five ships, of a combined tonnage of 2,140 were sent out to Fort St. George, containing, for the Fort, £14,832 in goods and £1,05,167 in bullion; for Masulipattinam, goods that could be sold there (the value is not specified) and £30,000 in bullion; and for Bengal, £23,000 in goods and £67,000 in bullion.[65] The value of the cargoes received in 1675 was £1,83,085 1s. 9d.[66] In 1708, the amount sent out in four ships to the 'Coast and Bay' was £3,00,000 in goods and bullion, of which £60,000 was to be invested on the coast and £2,40,000 in Bengal.[67] The following year, the total amount sent out had fallen to £2,60,000, of which £1,80,000 was for Bengal and the rest for the coast.[68] Obviously, they wanted the best possible deal for the Company even though investments on the coast had decreased considerably.

The factors, for their part, felt that they had no 'bad debts', and those that did exist, were 'made before that the Investments were undertaken by Tymona and Verona, in times of much less troubles then Since have been... '.[69] Besides, according to them the cloth provided by Viranna too was better, for he sent 'five of his own Servants unto each place being eighteene in number, having each their own circuits and severall others subdivided, with orders to looke after the business better and remedy what amiss ...'.[70] They further said that, but for Viranna's influence, no merchant would contract with the English. His and Timanna's heirs alone provided for a quarter of the Company's requirements.[71] Significantly, they also pointed out that Viranna was being wooed by the Dutch and the French.

Viranna was also involved in numerous other activities in and around Madras. He and Timanna had earlier built a 'Paddy Bancksall', and, in return, had collected a small fee on the paddy and rice brought into the town.[72] In 1676, he rented the paddy grounds at the rate of 40 pagodas per annum,[73] and was reported to have gone to considerable expense in 'clearing the Sand from the Sea wall'.[74] When the Company decided to levy a small charge of 2 *fanams* per house to recover the money they had paid in fortifications, 'all the Inhabitants nay their own Merchants all but Cassa Verona had shut up their shops ... [and] had stopped all provisions from coming to Towne ... '.[75] Viranna had taken up a number of revenue farms, such that he had almost the entire stretch of coast between Madras and Armagon in his hands (with the exception of Pulicat). He had been offered the district of Poonamallee, but had been induced to decline the offer, as it would have taken him off the Company's business.[76] In 1677, the Council reported that Kasi Viranna's town could annually make '4000 ordinary ginghams and 1000 fine ones',[77] which would seem to imply that he had enough weavers under his direct control to acquire that quantity of cloth.

The question of San Thomé, however, became a problematic one later, for Lingappa also wanted it. The terms of the grant were very similar to those granted to the English in Madras.[78] The town and its villages had been rented to Viranna for 1,500 pagodas per annum, but in 1679, Lingappa was given the farm for the same sum. This was because he had farmed the whole region for 2 lakh pagodas, and he declared that there was no possibility of getting that amount without San Thomé. 'Verona to prevent the inconvenience that may accrue to the Revenues of this Towne, by stoppage of Goods, Graine and the Callico Investment this yeare, hath writt to Golconda to use all meanes possible to wrest St. Thoma out of Lingapa's hands againe.'[79] In recognition of Viranna's importance and his services to the Company, it was decided to present him with a gold chain and a gold medal stamped with the Company's arms, 'to the value of £100'.[80] However, news of his death reached London before the chain could be presented, so orders were given to turn it into coins.

Viranna died on 20 March 1680, intestate. He had only one daughter. After his death, Lingappa demanded that 2,000 pagodas be paid to him by the new Chief Merchant, and declared that Viranna used to lend 6,000 pagodas per year, interest free, to the Divan; and 'if he that is now appointed our Chief Marchant will doe these things ..., we may doe our business with content'.[81] A little later, he also declared that as Viranna was dead, he would appoint a *havaldar* for Madras.

Viranna had been assisted by 'twenty six chief merchants, and many more below them', among whom were Timanna's brothers, Pedda and Chinna Venkatadri. In 1678, the latter had been imprisoned, following reports that he had 'exacted a tax from the Shopkeepers, Fishermen, Beetle and Tobacco merchants'. As he was also the head of the Peons in the Company's service, for which he was paid '100 fanams per mensem', it was decided to remove him from that post, 'whereby he may injure the Townes people, or under colour lead a party against the government'. He was involved in similar activities in other ports also, for he had 'command of the watch of ...Chycaracoat' (probably the modern town of Chicacole).[82] The other brother had, till then, received a small duty, for 'maintenance of the right hand Danceing Wenches, and, for the collecting the same, imploys a Concopla or Writer at the Choultry'. It was decided that he would no longer be entitled to that sum.[83] On Viranna's death, they were appointed to the post of Chief Merchants.

Viranna, in all his activities was Chief Merchant first, and everything else later. Though influential in the interior (but not to the extent that the Malaya family was, for he had no direct access to the court), his contact was more with the lower levels of administration, i.e. with those levels that comprised the extortionists. His value to the Company lay in the fact that he could deal comfortably with this level; but in any conflict, as for instance with Lingappa over San Thomé, it was the latter who was more likely to succeed. Thus, his influence was in the nature of reflected glory, for his rise to power was in Madras and because of Madras. His forays into revenue farming were more of a marginal nature, for the farms that he did take did not yield much.[84] By the 1670s, it was clear that Viranna had decided that his primary loyalty was to the English, whose interests he represented to the Golconda administration. This last included paying bribes out of his own pocket when necessary.[85]

The beginnings of the new equation between merchants, companies and the state had begun to be worked out under Timanna, and become more or less clarified under Viranna, reaching its final form under Viranna's successors. Pedda and Chinna Venkatadri were ordered to finalize accounts with all the merchants who had been involved in the trade with Viranna; but they declared that they had no knowledge of what Viranna had done, nor did they have the means to pay anything; and shortly afterwards, left town with the 'Pedda Naique and the Chief Painter with other Painters, the Muckwas, Cattamaran men and Cooleys'.[86] The Council ordered them to 'submit to Justice', failing which their 'houses, goods and Estate' would be confiscated. The brothers finally returned, and were imprisoned, but later released and allowed to join the joint stock that had been set up. Lingappa objected to their imprisonment, saying that no demands should be made on the two until they had been 'favoured' for four years, after which they would be able to satisfy all parties.[87] But not much notice was taken of what he said. Nevertheless, they did continue to trade on their own account, and also apparently had ships of their own. In fact mention is made of a ship *Tagraia* owned by Chinna Venkatadri and of 'several Pegu Merchants' arriving at Madras on one of his ships.[88]

Here is the first time that the subordination of the merchant to the Company becomes visible. As Company merchants, they were entitled to certain insignia of honour—to 'carry Rundells [and] have other things of honour', in the words of the factors—which were denied to other merchants living in the town. A visible difference was maintained between the Company's servants and others, in the Company's town. Such insignia would have perhaps been particularly important in the context of the changing political scenario, where, with increasing political instability, such markers of position and by extension, authority, were not otherwise easily acquired. Perhaps here, we can locate the origins of the British establishing their role as dispensers of legitimacy.

Significantly, these rules were enforced despite an individual, Lingappa, the local *tarafdar*, demanding that the same concessions that had been granted earlier be continued, and further that the brothers be 'favoured' for a period of at least four years. The assumption being that within those four years, they would have been able to strengthen their base to such an extent that the Company would not have been able to do anything against them—precisely what the Company wanted to avoid. Unable to take any action against Viranna, or prevent his virtual monopoly, company officials were trying their best to prevent a recurrence of the same problem. It is a different matter that a change in the Governor led to a change in policy—for the new Governor, William Gyfford, reinstated the brothers. Nevertheless, it must be pointed out here that the control that the British were beginning to assert, at least over those forts that they possessed, was starting to take shape. Further extension of this attitude can be seen a little later on the west coast when, in the 1720s, after the trouble with Kanhoji Angré, the British began legal proceedings against Dulba Bhandari, a resident and merchant of Bombay, for being a traitor to the British, and supposedly supplying information to Kanhoji about the state of affairs at Bombay.

The seventeenth and early eighteenth centuries contain frequent references to Makhdum Nina, a merchant and shipowner of Porto Novo, and to the competition he offered to the English at Fort St. David.[89] In 1691, he was reported to have 'brought his family and Shipping to Settle at Cuddalore'. In return for his having been 'very industrious and Serviceable' in drawing other rich merchants to settle there, as well as the expenses he incurred in fortifying the town, it was decided that he be 'commissioned Captaine of the Chuliars Moors and Gentue...'.[90] Later, he reported that he had spent 1,700 pagodas on a present to Daud Khan, on the Company's account.[91] This resulted in some problems between the Company and Makhdum Nina, for the latter had been told in no uncertain terms that he should not spend more than 300 pagodas. Concentrated efforts were made to get him to settle at Fort St. David, in the hope that he would boost the declining trade there;[92] in turn, he wanted assurances from them about free and fair trade and religious freedom, which the English were quite prepared to grant. Ultimately, he never did move to Fort St. David.

The Dutch experience was rather different. After their experiences with Malaya and Chinanna, they stopped giving their contracts to any one merchant, but instead to a large number of merchants. In the 1670s, they were reported to owe large sums of money on the coast, but did not pay any interest on it. The money was owed to the merchants from whom they bought their goods, and so, the merchants merely 'over rated their goods by 30 to 40%'.[93] Chinanna's departure for the kingdom of Thanjavur had resulted in numerous problems for the Dutch, not the least of which was bad debts. Another problem was the quality of cloth, and the quantities required. Early on, the Dutch had realized that the quantities they needed meant that a larger number of merchants had to supply the same varieties of cloth—which meant more advances, greater competition among the merchants, which would lead to higher prices, and a correspondingly greater likelihood of bad debts.

The Dutch were the first to establish formal partnerships, or joint stocks, among Indian merchants. The first attempts at a joint stock were made under Laurens Pit, the Dutch Governor of the Coromandel from 1652–63. He began with merchants supplying a variety of cloth sold in the Moluccas known as 'ternate cloth'.[94] These merchants were asked to band together in an association, so that they would no longer compete among themselves. The result was a dramatic improvement in the quality of cloth, and so Pit went on to form three more such associations, two for longcloth or 'Guinea cloth', and another for embroidered muslins.[95] Similarly, the Dutch introduced other joint stocks among their settlements along the coast. Their example was followed by the English at Madras after Viranna's death, in 1680, as also by the French at Pondicherri.

Two rather conflicting opinions have been expressed about the joint stocks. One is that of Brennig, who views it as 'an early instance of the attempted transfer of a basically European commercial institution to a non-Western economic environment'.[96] Arasaratnam, on the other hand, believes that the 'concept of the joint stock must certainly have been prevalent in some form in the merchant guilds that flourished under the Vijayanagar Empire'.[97] It should be remembered that these Indian joint stocks were not independent organizations, nor were they a logical development of the trends in India. Rather, they were associations created by the Europeans to serve their own needs, and so were carefully watched over by them. They were, therefore, a means of exercising control over the Indian merchants, so as to increase the profits of the Company concerned.

The total capital of the stock was fixed according to the means of the merchants involved. Then the duties were divided among the chief shareholders. In 1688, the English set up a joint stock consisting of 12 head merchants, of whom two were responsible for the seals of the stock and for calling meetings, two were in charge of the cash, three others looked after the textile trade, two were in charge of the goods imported from Europe, and the remaining three were in charge of the artisans. Junior merchants were required to go into the country to supervise the work of the weavers.[98] At the end of the year, the accounts of the company were finalized, and dividends declared 'for each shareholder who then received the amount due to him after deduction of what he had drawn from the common fund'.[99] The total capital of the stocks varied between 1,50,000 pagodas at the highest and about 1,00,000 pagodas at the lowest.[100]

During the tenure of Pit's successor, Cornelius Speelman, such joint stocks were formed in most of the Dutch factories, but with varied results; so that, in north Coromandel, such associations began to come into existence only after 1680. At Nagapattinam, the process was even slower, with the first joint stock being established only in 1689.[101] The Indian merchants in the joint stocks had both rights and obligations. Of the former, the most important was the exclusive right to the import and export trade of the European companies, with preference being given to those who could complete their investments in time. Of the latter, the most significant was the concept of collective responsibility, something that was not always accepted when large sums were involved. For instance, at Fort St. George, a joint stock led by Chikka Serappa fell into debt, but the merchants could not decide among themselves about its settlement. Serappa offered to pay his proportion, but was told that 'there was no proportion in a joint stock'.[102] Serappa was imprisoned for a while, but to no effect. He complained that his imprisonment had 'so much prejudiced his Credits in the Country that it hindred the bringing in the Goods to finish the last contract...'.[103] Later, the joint stock broke up, with the English forced to accept proportionate repayment.

The primary European advantage of the joint stock was that it dispensed with the need to make large advances to the merchants, for the joint stock itself was made responsible for the advances. But such contracts could really work only so long as there were wealthy and influential merchants who could provide the major portion of the stock, and who could supervise the junior merchants. Given the factor of increasing dependence on European trade and the growing difficulties faced in investment as a result of wars and famine, the number of wealthy and influential merchants began to decline. Also, 'influential' in the seventeenth and in the eighteenth centuries meant different things, so that, an influential merchant of the seventeenth century was one who had influence with the local governments, while in the eighteenth century, such merchants were those who had influence within the European enclaves. In the case of Madras, from 1720, concern began to be expressed about the steadily declining trade, which meant that the merchants drew nearer to the factors in their private trade, rather than in the Company trade. It was from this time that the feature, so common in the late eighteenth and nineteenth centuries, began to take shape, where all rich Englishmen, whether merchant or official, had their own personal *dubashes*.[104] The joint stocks were often 'dominated by one or two merchants who provided all the capital and put their relatives and servants as partners'.[105] This naturally limited the amount of money they could put into the stock, and therefore, undermined a basic reason for establishing the joint stocks, that of reducing advances. In the context of the increasing instability of the early eighteenth century, no merchant, whether as an individual or as part of the joint stock, could be persuaded to tie himself down to a specific contract.

In some ways, the English found it easier than the Dutch to recover bad debts, for at Madras, the merchants were allowed to buy houses and land, something that the Dutch did not permit. The monopolistic control of the Dutch, as opposed to the freedom at Madras, also tended to draw more merchants to the latter. Pondicherri under the French also drew a large number of Indian merchants,[106] but of the three (i.e. Pulicat, Madras and Pondicherri), Madras grew fastest, and largest in terms of merchants, while Pondicherri attracted the largest number of weavers, who came as a result of the French reputation for paying reasonable prices. This process picked up momentum after the 1730s, when the French investment increased.[107] At Madras, the only successful experiment at establishing a weaving village was Chintadripetta in 1734, which was initiated by two merchants, Vennala Narayana Chetti and Chinnathambi Mudaliar.[108]

As mentioned earlier, European trade was considered to be beneficial to an area. In 1682, for instance, a letter was received from Gopal Pandit, the subedar of Porto Novo, offering the English a *qaul* to settle at Porto Novo and Kunimedu, to 'augment the Diwan's Profitts ... and encrease the Place ...'.[109] The English wrote back, asking for some more concessions, on the same lines as those enjoyed by the French at Pondicherri, but were told that nothing 'more than what was agreed of at first' was possible.[110]

Mughal conquest disrupted the existing patterns, and problems continued to affect the trade of the coast until after the end of the century. For instance, in 1695, it was reported that the revolt of the Telugu Rajas had affected the trade of Vishakhapattinam and Masulipattinam. Two attempts had been made to 'plunder Vizagapatam', and only timely action by the English factory there had repulsed the raiders. Vishakhapattinam was reported to be 'the only place in all those parts which has not submitted to the Rajahs ...'.[111] The Mughal official was reported to be grateful for this, but not to the extent of allowing the English to fortify their factory.

The final years of the century saw coastal trade being severely affected, not only because of the wars, but also due to a general famine. The Europeans found that only the slave trade was flourishing, because starving people came to the ports to sell themselves. The situation began to improve in the early years of the eighteenth century. Once again, trade began from Madras; and a somewhat novel tangent which was beginning to be explored was that to China. In 1702, some inhabitants of Madras fitted out 'two small Country ships, with considerable stocks ...'.[112] The Company too decided to lease out one of their ships to these merchants, so as to provide them with a small degree of protection.

Aurangzeb's death upset the delicate balance once again. The English were quick to note that the government had 'in Generall ... grown much weaker', for 'none of the great men keep up the number of Horse allowed by the King, but apply the money to their own use ...'.[113] The effect was, on the one hand, to intensify the attempts at control by the local officials, and on the other, the tacit acceptance on the part of the Europeans of the need for force to maintain their position. This acceptance had steadily been increasing for the last two decades of the seventeenth century, and mention has been made earlier of the vigorous defence of Fort St. David by the English. The security that the European fortified settlements offered had been clear to the Indian rulers for a long time; as was stated earlier, Mir Jumla's treasure was stored at Pulicat, and on Bahadur Shah's death, 'several considerable persons came down from Arcott with great sums of money to be lodg'd within our walls ...'.[114] The Mughal officials took advantage of this security, but tried in various ways to wrest more control over the settlements. Sa'adatullah Khan captured Jinji in 1714, and then declared that Cuddalore and the other towns near Fort St. David were part of his jagir, and had to be given up to him. The English protested, saying that their title to all these areas was clear, unlike that of the French at Pondicherri, for they had purchased the towns well before the Mughal conquest. But they were aware of the vulnerability of their position, for the passage of goods into the towns could be easily stopped. The necessity of defending their trade increasingly prompted the Europeans to be aggressors rather than defenders; an aggression that had to be against European competitors as well as Indian rulers. For the English, the support of the latter was necessary to ensure the end of European competition, and so, the French and the English steadily began to involve themselves in the politics of the courts of the various Indian rulers.

On the other hand, it must also be pointed out that the Indian merchants did make many attempts to retain their independence, and were to a great extent supported by the new rulers. Early in the eighteenth century Sa'adatullah Khan was reported to be trying to create a new port, to which he hoped to be able to draw the Indian merchants.[115] From the records, it appears that the Nawab was, in some measure, taking over the role that had earlier been played by the larger empires, that of promoting and protecting Indian trade and traders. Porto Novo retained its role as the port from which Indian shipping continued its operations, and in the eighteenth century, the most important route was the one to Manila. This trade was, by all accounts, dominated by the Indian merchants, along with some Portuguese, and certain Company officials in their private capacity as traders. Indian shipping from this port was free of all European restraints, other than that of taking passes for the movement of ships. Makhdum Nina was one of those involved in this trade.

The Philippine Trade

Broadly speaking, the trade to the Philippines can be divided into four categories. The first was that of the individual merchant, into which category include merchants like Makhdum Nina. I have already discussed English efforts to woo him, offering him the protection of the fort (Fort St. David), and making him the chief of the soldiers defending the fort at the time of the Mughal attacks. Apparently the English also owed him a large sum of money though this is none too clear, for the English stated that he had offered to pay the soldiers on his own account, but the latter claimed that he had been ordered to do so. He and his sons traded regularly from Porto Novo to Manila, as well as to some of the islands in the Indonesian archipelago. The value of his trade is never mentioned, but from the records of customs duties that his ships paid, it appears that he was a fairly wealthy merchant. Despite repeated attempts, he did not finally move to the British settlement, preferring to trade out of Port Novo itself. After his death, his sons-in-law continued to trade from the same port, but do not seem to have met with as much success as their father-in-law. In contrast to the four ships said to have been owned by Makhdum Nina, his sons were reported to have only one, and to have freighted their goods on Armenian ships.

The next category comprised the Armenians, the single major group trading to Manila. The earliest mention of the trade to Manila comes from the late seventeenth century, when the factors at Madras reported the arrival of a ship (from Manila) belonging to an Armenian merchant at Madras. The ship would most probably have been a small one, for the tonnage is not mentioned, but the cargo included oil and timber. In return, the Armenian merchant was planning to take cotton cloth and European goods, including broadcloth.[116] Subsequently, there is mention of at least one or two ships belonging to this merchant in each shipping season.

The third group involved in the trade to Manila were the Portuguese. Many Portuguese had settled down in Madras, where they found occupation mainly as soldiers in the English army. However, there were still more who had long been settled at the Portuguese settlement of San Thomé, who joined hands with Indian merchants to trade to the Philippines. This trade was definitely not a very large one, in terms of either goods or money, for references in the Mayor's court proceedings record debts of 50 pagodas being owed on voyages to Manila.[117]

The fourth group were the East India Company merchants trading in their private capacity. From the first and second decades of the eighteenth century, there are frequent references to merchants of Madras travelling to Manila. One case in the Mayor's court involved a debt, to a Portuguese resident of Madras by an Indian merchant residing in Manila—the case in question was the non-payment of 25 barrels of oil which the Indian merchant had promised to supply, but did not. Interestingly, the Portuguese merchant, by the time the case actually came up in the court, had shifted to Calcutta, and was plying his trade from there. He sent, as his representative in the court, the brother of the merchant from whom he was claiming the money.[118]

In yet another case, a Portuguese trader in Madras had died, and left in his widow's hands large sums of money belonging to Indian and Portuguese merchants involved in the Manila trade. The court demanded that a representative from the Manila end of the business be present in Madras, and fixed a date for the hearing in two months time—proof enough, if one wanted it, that someone could go to Manila, deliver the summons, and be back within two months.[119] This also testifies to the regularity of the trade contacts, and to the fact that the British were well aware of the same, but either did not, or could not, interfere.

It is possible that it was the latter rather than the former. In the early years of the eighteenth century, the British also were in none too happy a situation. The French had emerged as serious rivals; and the insecurity in the peninsula, as well as the recurring famines, had adversely affected the supply of goods for the European markets. Also, at least in the earlier decades, the Nawab of Arcot's attempts to establish a port within his own dominions also played a part. It is probably significant that, once the British had assured their position in the south, they did send out, first a scouting expedition to the Philippines, and later, a war party. By the close of 1768, Manila was in British hands. For some years after that, trade between Porto Novo in particular and Manila seems to have continued, but by the 1780s, colonial rule had been firmly established. The trade then dwindled to merely peddling trade, in small ships, and for small quantities.

Notes

1. E. Thurston, *Castes and Tribes of Southern India*, Madras, 1909, vol. III, p. 306.
2. Many of them are now jewellers.
3. V. Ramaswamy, *Textiles and Weavers in Medieval South India*, New Delhi: Oxford University Press, 1985, p. 58.
4. Francis Buchanan, *A Journey from Madras through the Countries of Mysore, Canara and Malabar in the year 1800*, London: Cadell and Davies, 1807, p. 77.
5. Records of Fort St. George, *Diary and Consultation Books* (henceforth *RFSG, Diary*), 26 August 1707, in which details of settlement of 1652 are given; H.D. Love, ed., *Vestiges of Old Madras*, 3 vols., London, 1913 (henceforth *Vestiges*), vol. I, pp. 118–19; vol. II, pp. 25–30; W. Foster, ed., *The English Factories in India* (henceforth *EFI*), Oxford: Clarendon Press, 1906–27, n.s., ed., C. Fowcett, 4 vols., *EFI*, 1651–4, p. 155 and *passim.*
6. RFSG, *Despatches to England*, 22 December 1707.
7. *Vestiges*, vol. I, p. 120.
8. Ibid.; *EFI*, 1651–4, p. 155 and *passim.*
9. *Annual Report on South Indian Epigraphy* (henceforth *ARSIE*), 363 of 1907.
10. M.L. Dames, tr. and ed., *The Book of Duarte Barbosa*, 2 vols., London: Hakluyt Society, 1918, vol. II, p. 175. According to him, one *bahar* was equal to 448 lbs. Cf. ibid., vol. I, 157, fn 1.
11. B.A. Saletore, 'Some Aspects of the Overseas Trade of Vijayanagar from the Accounts of European Travellers', in *B.C. Law Commemoration Volume*, ed. D.R. Bhandarkar, Calcutta, 1945, p. 124.
12. W.H. Moreland, ed., *Relations of Golconda in the Early Seventeenth Century*, London: Hakluyt Society, 1931, p. 36.
13. *EFI*, 1642–5, p. 130.
14. Ibid., 1618–21, p. 281.
15. Ibid., 1661–4, p. 179.
16. Lady Fawcett, tr., and Charles Fawcett, ed., *The Travels of the Abbé Carré in India and the Near East, 1672–1674*, London: Hakluyt Society, 1947–8; New Delhi: Asian Educational Services, rpt, 1990, 2 vols., vol. I, p. 18.
17. RFSG, *Diary*, 28 June 1688. However, we do have some references to brokers prior to this, for there are references in inscriptions to *taragu kasu*, which is taken to mean brokerage fee. See A. Appadorai, *Economic Conditions in Southern India, AD 1000–1500*, 2 vols., Madras: University of Madras, 1936, vol. II, p. 72.
18. RFSG, *Diary*, 28 September 1675.
19. Ibid.

20. Ibid., 11 March 1706.
21. *Masulipatnam Factory Records*, vol. 2, consultation of August 1678; also cited by J. Irwin, and P.R. Schwartz, *Studies in Indo-European Textile History*, Ahmedabad: Calico Museum of Textiles, 1966.
22. S. Arasaratnam, *Merchants, Companies and Commerce on the Coromandel Coast, 1650–1750*, Delhi: Oxford University Press, 1986, p. 222.
23. J.J. Brennig, 'Chief Merchants and the European Enclaves of 17th Century Coromandel', *Modern Asian Studies*, nos. 2 and 3, 1977, pp. 321–40.
24. V. Ramaswamy, *Textiles and Weavers* ..., op. cit., p. 314.
25. J.J. Brennig, 'Chief Merchants ...', op. cit.
26. S. Arasaratnam, '*Merchants*, ...', op. cit., p. 222.
27. Ibid., p. 223.
28. The records tend to be rather confusing, for they refer to Malaya and Chinanna as one and the same person. However, it appears that Malaya died around 1636, and the position that he had occupied was taken over by his brother.
29. J.J. Brennig, op. cit.
30. S. Arasaratnam, op. cit., p. 223.
31. *EFI*, 1642–5, p. 154.
32. *Vestiges*, vol. I, p. 64, RFSG, *Letter from Fort St. George to Surat*, 8 September 1645.
33. Ibid., p. 45. This led to some hostility between Pulicat and Fort St. George, but closer links between the English and Vijayanagar through Sesadri Chetti, the English Chief Merchant and a member of the Malaya family. It was at this time that the English got their grant of Madras reconfirmed by Sriranga.
34. S. Arasaratnam, op. cit., p. 223.
35. It has been suggested by J.J. Brennig that as the political role of these merchants was entwined with the 'Hindu' political structure, they were bound to suffer from the expansion of the Muslim kingdoms. However, more studies of this aspect need to be undertaken, for it implies that trade had to be aligned differently to suit different religions; or alternatively, that state policies were defined by religion, which does not seem to be the case. See J.J. Brennig, op. cit.
36. K.A.N. Sastri, *South India and Southeast Asia: Studies in their History and Culture*, Mysore: Geetha Book House, 1978, pp. 202–3.
37. K.A.N. Sastri, *History of South India*, 3rd edn, Madras, 1966, pp. 248–52.
38. Ibid.
39. J.N. Sarkar, *The Life of Mir Jumla, the General of Aurangzeb*, 2nd revd. edn, New Delhi, 1979.
40. *Vestiges*, vol. I. p. 76.
41. *EFI*, 1646–50, p. 166. He first lent 16,000 rials of eight, and then 10,000 pagodas, and the English continued to be in his debt from March 1646 to June 1647.
42. Ibid., 1651–4, p. 12.
43. Ibid., p. 22.
44. Ibid., 1655–60, p. 92.

45. S. Arasaratnam, op. cit., p. 225.
46. T. Raychaudhuri, *Jan Company in Coromandel Coast, 1605–1690: A Study in the Interrelations of European Commerce and Traditional Economics*, The Hague, 1962, p. 121.
47. *Vestiges*, vol. I, p. 64.
48. Ibid., p. 144.
49. Ibid., p. 122.
50. *EFI*, 1661–4, p. 165.
51. RFSG, *Diary*, 2 September 1680.
52. *Vestiges*, vol. I, p. 128.
53. J.J. Brennig, op. cit.
54. RFSG, *Diary*, 27 November 1678.
55. R.C. Temple, ed., *The Diaries of Streynsham Master*, op. cit., vol. I, p. 77; vol. II, p. 152.
56. C. Fawcett, *The Travels of the Abbé Carré*, vol. II, pp. 605 and 610.
57. *Vestiges*, vol. I, p. 231.
58. RFSG, *Diary*, 14 June 1672.
59. RFSG, *Diary*, 14 September 1676.
60. Ibid.
61. RFSG, *Despatches from England*, 8 January 1674.
62. E.B. Sainsbury, ed., *A Calendar of the Court Minutes, etc. of the East India Company*, Oxford: Clarendon Press, 1907, p. 374, minutes of 10 November 1679.
63. RFSG, *Despatches from England, Letter to Fort St. George*, 15 December 1676.
64. *EFI*, n.s., vol. II, p. 143.
65. RFSG, *Despatches from England, Letter to Fort St. George*, 24 December 1675.
66. E.B. Sainsbury, *Court Minutes*, op. cit., p. 135.
67. RFSG, *Despatches from England, Letter to Fort St. George*, 4 February 1708.
68. Ibid., 9 January 1709.
69. RFSG, *Diary*, 29 February 1676.
70. Ibid., 28 September 1675.
71. Ibid., 7 May 1675.
72. Ibid., 18 February 1676.
73. *EFI*, n.s., vol. II, p. 146.
74. RFSG, *Diary*, 29 February 1676.
75. Ibid.
76. *EFI*, n.s., vol. II, p. 146.
77. Ibid., p. 176.
78. Ibid.
79. RFSG, *Diary*, 31 August 1679.
80. E.B. Sainsbury, op. cit., 4 November 1679.
81. Ibid., 15 September 1680.
82. R.C. Temple, ed., *The Diaries of Streynsham Master*, op. cit., vol. I, *Journey from Fort St. George to Masulipatnam*; also RFSG, *Diary*, 13 March 1679.

83. Ibid., 25 November 1678.
84. According to Master, he had taken the farm of Armagon's customs, which were no more than 60 pagodas per annum, and San Thomé gave him only the 1,500 pagodas for which he had rented it. R.C. Temple, ed., op. cit., vol. I, p. 77.
85. *Vestiges*, vol. I, pp. 90–1, 391–2, and *passim*.
86. RFSG, *Diary*, 26 October 1680.
87. *EFI*, n.s., vol. IV, p. 27.
88. RFSG, *Diary*, 25 March 1686 and 13 April 1686.
89. RFSG, *Diary*, 9 July 1691.
90. Ibid.
91. Ibid., 7 October 1703.
92. Chief of Fort St. David to Directors, 1710–11—cited by S. Arasaratnam, op. cit., p. 220.
93. R.C. Temple, ed., op. cit., vol. I, p. 297.
94. J.J. Brennig, 'Joint Stock Companies of Coromandel', in *The Age of Partnership: Europeans in Asia Before Dominion*, B.B. Kling and M.N. Pearson, eds., pp. 71–94.
95. S. Arasaratnam, op. cit., p. 240.
96. J.J. Brennig, 'Joint Stock …', op. cit.
97. S. Arasaratnam, 'Indian Merchants and their Trading Methods, *c.*1700', *Indian Economic and Social History Review*, vol. 3, no. 1, 1966, pp. 85–95.
98. RFSG, *Diary*, 19 April 1688.
99. S. Arasaratnam, '*Merchants*, …', op. cit., p. 244.
100. S. Arasaratnam, 'Indian Merchants …', op. cit., p. 87.
101. S. Arasaratnam, '*Merchants*, …', op. cit., p. 247.
102. RFSG, *Fort St. David Consultations*, 9 September 1703 and 11 October 1703.
103. RFSG, *Diary*, 11 October 1703.
104. Susan Nield-Basu, 'The Dubashes of Madras', *Modern Asian Studies*, 1987, pp. 1–31.
105. S. Arasaratnam, '*Merchants*, …', op. cit., p. 214.
106. J.F. Price and K. Rangachari, eds., *The Private Diary of Ananda Ranga Pillai, Dubash to Joseph Francois Dupleix, Governor of Pondicherry*, 12 vols., Madras: Government Press, 1904–28, vol. I, p. 119, says that 'The Brahmans, Komattis and Tattuvadis who flocked into Pondicherri from morning until evening of this day, from Arcot, Vellore and Wandiwash, and other places, might exceed 1,000 in number.'
107. RFSG, *Despatches to England*, 1 October 1733.
108. *Vestiges*, vol. II, pp. 259–61.
109. RFSG, *Letters to Fort St. George*, 12 January 1682.
110. Ibid., March 1682.
111. RFSG, *Despatches to England*, 3 April 1695.
112. RFSG, *Diary*, 22 May 1702.
113. RFSG, *Despatches to England*, 22 December 1711.
114. Ibid., 14 October 1712.

115. Muzaffar Alam and Sanjay Subrahmanyam, 'Exploring the Hinterland: Trade and Politics in the Arcot Nizamat (1700–1732)', in *Politics and Trade in the Indian Ocean World: Essays in Honour of Ashin Das Gupta*, Rudrangshu Mukherjee and Laksmi Subramaniam, eds., Delhi: Oxford University Press, 1998, pp. 113–64, esp. pp. 148–52.
116. RFSG, *Diary*, 6 June 1692.
117. RFSG, *Proceedings in the Mayor's Court*, 1727.
118. Ibid., 12 September 1727.
119. Ibid., 26 September 1727. The sum of pagodas 1785.17.21 was in her hands.

CHAPTER 4

'Our Fort and City'

THE ENGLISH had established their headquarters at Armagon near Pulicat in 1626. To begin with, it showed considerable promise, and the English factors wrote to the Court of Directors in London stating that they had been successful in inducing weavers to come and settle in their vicinity. But these welcome beginnings were short-lived, and by 1632, the factors had began to report that business at Armagon was getting more difficult. This was in part due to natural causes because that year saw unseasonal and heavy rainfall, but much more because of warfare. They began to complain that the fort was dilapidated and a large expenditure on repair though unavoidable, would likely be pointless because the harbour was shallow and exposed and smaller boats too found it difficult to come near the shore. Perhaps also as a result of increasing warfare, the local Nayak had begun to be much more demanding and increasingly unfriendly. The search therefore began for a new place in which to settle.

As the primary interest was textiles and their export, the main criterion dictating the choice of a place had to be: (1) availability of textiles, (2) reasonable port facilities, and after that, (3) a local ruler who did not place too many hindrances in the way of trade. The English believed that most coastal Nayaks would be inclined to encourage trade from which they derived their major income—an idea that continued its hold even after the experience with the Nayak of Armagon.

In 1637, Francis Day, the chief factor at Armagon, undertook a voyage of exploration as far south as Pondicherri. This expedition ultimately led to overtures from Damarla Venkatapati (or Venkatadri) who, according to the English, was the Nayak of Kalahasti, and controlled the coast between Pulicat and San Thomé. He himself spent considerable time at the court of the Vijayanagar king while his dominions were governed by his brother who based himself at Poonamallee.[1]

In words that are reminiscent of the way in which Armagon had been described earlier, the future site of Fort St. George was also said to produce 'the best paintings ..., or as good as anywhere on this coast ... and better Cheape by 20 percent then anywhere else'.[2] The land that was actually granted was a small island, which lay in the middle of two branches of the river, known locally as *narimedu* or fox's ground. It was fairly close to the historic port of Mailapur, possibly that which had been known to Roman traders as Mylarpha, but by now a not very important port. It was about 8 km. from the Portuguese settlement of San Thomé, something that the English were not too concerned with. According to the terms of the grant for the settlement the English would be allowed to build a fort, the charges for which would be borne by the Nayak, provided the amount was repaid when the English took possession of the fort. However, the Nayak later claimed that he had made no such offer and did not contribute anything towards building expenses.[3] The English were given the authority to govern the new settlement including the right to levy and collect revenues. For the first two years, all the income was to be taken by the English and thereafter, was to be equally divided between the Company and the Nayak. The Company's goods sold at Fort St. George were to be entirely and permanently duty-free and in addition, the Company was to pay only half the regular inland tolls in the Nayak's territories. The Company was also granted mint facilities in the town, on condition of payment of 'the regular wages' to those who coined the money. In return, the Nayak undertook responsibility for the fulfilment of contracts by the weavers and other artisans, provided he was first consulted as to their trustworthiness. He also demanded that the English supply him with horses from Persia—presumably at concessional rates.

For the last, we do not know whether the English fulfilled their part of the contract. No mention is made of whether horses were ever imported for the Nayak. In fact, the records do not mention horses as an item of import at any time. Interestingly the English claimed that they had been granted permission to build a fort because the Nayak had hoped to be able to use it as a refuge in times of need; but before the fort had been completed, the Nayak had been imprisoned by the king and we find no further mention of him in the records. By 1648, the area had come under the control of Golconda, and Mallappa, an agent of that government, was stationed at the fort between 1648 and 1654 to collect the half-share of the revenue. This, the earliest of the English possessions in India, soon developed a distinct identity.

The establishment and the development of the European settlements on the Coromandel Coast in the seventeenth century (though this was much more an eighteenth century process) took place at approximately the same pace as the decline of the Indian states. The development of the city of Madras is, perhaps, illustrative of the way in which the English began to provide an alternative to the Indian merchants, in more ways than one. Prior to their arrival, the place had been, if not deserted, then nearly so, for it was merely one of the innumerable fishing villages that dotted the coast. The area had been well known in ancient times, for as mentioned earlier

Mailapur was in the vicinity of the new fort. In the seventeenth century it was known for its proximity to San Thomé. (Today, it is one of the most crowded parts of Chennai). San Thomé itself was a Portuguese establishment, which was, successively, in the kingdoms of Thanjavur and Golconda, then in the hands of the French, and then Golconda again. Later in the century, it was farmed out, first to Kasi Viranna, and then to the Company, through another of its merchants. Late in the seventeenth century, it once again became a Portuguese possession, but was linked more to the private trade of the Portuguese than to the Estado.[4]

The area nearest the Fort soon came to be known as White Town, for other than the official buildings, the residences of the Governor, the Council members and the other Englishmen were also located there. White Town was laid out in what can perhaps be called European fashion, in that its layout was much more evocative of the European fortified towns. Roughly a rectangle, it was initially limited to the island that was first granted. The fort was the centre of the settlement. At the mouth of the river, and overlooked by the fort, was the harbour. The mint, customs house and the choultry (which was both the place where land customs were collected and became a court of justice when needed) were also built near the fort. Not too many houses were originally built inside this part of the town, for it reflected the primary purpose of a fortified settlement for trade. White Town was fortified in stages, and, as and when necessary, the walls were strengthened, and within about twenty years of the original grant, walls completely encircled White Town. In the interest of easy defence, no houses or other establishments were allowed near the walls, and a clear stretch of ground was ordered to be maintained all around the fort. In the early eighteenth century, in fact, homes which had come up too near the walls were ordered to be demolished. The idea was to make Fort St. George and the nearby town strong enough to withstand any assault, whether by an 'Indian prince' or by 'ye Dutch power of India if we should happen to have any difference with them hereafter ...'.[5]

Eventually, as the Company's hold over the town grew, and as English trade became more firmly established, houses of the Company officials began to come up inside. Towards the end of the century, the factors wrote to London, asking whether rich merchants could be allowed to go to and from the fort as free merchants. The Court of Directors replied that they would consider the matter, and approved of the factors' 'design of Inviteing rich Banians and China merchants, to live at the ffort', calling it a 'prudent and generous' move.[6] Many of the Company servants gradually began to buy land outside the town, so that the European idea of a 'house in the country' also began to make its appearance in India. By the middle of the eighteenth century, suburbs also developed. To start with, the suburbs were the villages that had gradually been added to the original grant, and which retained their distinct identity. Roads inside White Town were clearly marked and laid out, and shortly after the English occupied the place, a church was built. A Protestant church, it had its own cemetery close by, in which Englishmen (and women) were buried. Catholics had their own church outside White Town, as had the Armenians. For quite a long time, the Catholic church was under two French Capuchin fathers, who began to be regarded with a degree of suspicion only after 1672, when the French occupied San Thomé.

For the defence of the town, a small militia was raised, consisting mainly of Portuguese soldiers, under the command of an English captain. The Portuguese were considered advantageous in more ways than one, for not only did they provide soldiers, but as many had been born and brought up in India, and had often married Indian women, their knowledge of local languages and customs could be tapped when necessary. White Town remained clearly distinct until the end of the eighteenth century, when, after British rule had been firmly established, the walls were broken down in order to allow the settlement to grow.

North of White Town lay the Indian part of the settlement, known variously as Black Town, Chinnapattinam (from which name we get the present Chennai), Madraspattinam, or Madras. Initially, there was no clear demarcation between White Town and Black Town, but, as mentioned earlier, as White Town began to be gradually enclosed by walls, the division grew sharper. Twenty years after the first settlement, the two parts were clearly and separately identifiable. However, the British claimed that both parts of the settlement were under their jurisdiction, for both together made their 'fort and city of Madraspatam'. In the course of the century, and particularly from the 1670s, they consolidated their hold over Black Town as well, and asserted their right to govern it according to their requirements and concerns.

In 1674, the factors were asked to try and collect a 'Quit rent for the houses in the Town', but to be very 'cautious of causing any disorder or discontent among the inhabitants ...'.[7] By 1682, however, the tone of the instructions had changed. Now, they said that, by 'Dutch Portuguese or Indian methods' sufficient revenue should be raised at Madras to 'defray at least the whole constant charge of the place'.[8] Shortly after, the Court of Directors recommended that Black Town should also be 'walled round and completely fortified at the charge of the Inhabitants, whether it please or displease them or anyone else ...'.[9] This resulted in an immediate uproar in Black Town, where the inhabitants 'did ... tumultuously and mutinously combine together, commanding the Severall Casts to desist from their labour, & service to us ...'.[10] Earlier, too, a similar occurrence had taken place, for when an attempt was made to collect 230 pagodas from the inhabitants of Black Town,[11] 'all but Cassa Verona [Kasi Viranna] had shut up their shops

& gathered up to ye pagoda, and by intelligence their Tribes in the country had stopped all provisions from coming to Towne, . . . They did not value the summe, but the Precedent'.[12] At that time, for fear that the merchants and others would leave the town, the factors had backed down. Barely ten years later, they declared that the merchants were free to leave the town if they did not want to pay the dues towards fortifying Black Town. In fact, 'Soldiers were drawn out ... to suppress the Tumult ...', and they were told that, if they stopped goods entering the town, they would be 'sought out and punished'.[13]

The change in the British attitude is clear indication of the decreasing support that the merchants were able to muster within the region. In 1676, Golconda still existed, as an independent and fairly strong empire. Madanna, Akkanna, and the various members of their family were, no doubt, regarded as the major oppressors of the Europeans, but the fact remained that, for the Indian merchants, they were the representatives of a traditional political structure. As has been mentioned earlier, after Viranna's death, Lingappa came out in favour of Pedda and Chinna Venkatadri, saying that they should be 'favoured' for four years. Simultaneously, Akkanna threatened to destroy the Company's trade at Golconda, unless the brothers were restored to their position as chief merchants.[14] Earlier, when the brothers had got into trouble in Madras, over non-payment of their debts, they fled from Madras to Lingappa's camp.

In 1686, the Golconda Sultanate's continued existence came under serious threat. Lingappa and other officials of the same level were, no doubt, still present, but lacked the backing of a solid state structure, and thus did not have any real power to force the Europeans to do as they desired. The merchants, therefore, had to work out other, newer, equations, and given the political turmoil that afflicted the south for the next two decades, these equations had to include the Europeans. It is in this context that one has to see the recurrence of caste disputes in Madras and other places along the coast, for the first time since 1652. Black Town was the scene of the caste disputes in 1652, 1707 and ten years later again in 1717.

In 1707, a fight broke out in Black Town between the left- and right-hand castes, and the Governor of the fort was forced to 'order Guards to lye out to keep the Peace ...'.[15] The Council decided, as in 1652, to try to solve the problem, and so as an initial measure, Black Town was surveyed, and 'a Draught of all the Streets and Buildings in the Petta' was drawn up. It was found that the demarcation of 1652 had become rather unclear, and some of the right-hand had built their houses in the streets belonging to the left. They were then ordered to sell their houses and move back to their own streets. To ensure that 'neither Cast may pretend Ignorance of their limits', it was ordered that four boundary stones be set up, with the orders 'inscribed thereon in English and Gentue'.[16]

This did not solve the problem, and in August it was reported that many of the right-hand had left the town. The Governor then 'summoned Twelve of the Principall Heads of each Cast' and shut them up in a room in the fort to discuss and settle matters.[17]

The main problem was not that of streets or houses, but the fact that the right-hand castes felt that they were not being favoured as much as the left. Such events were not stray; similar caste disputes occurred at other places along the coast, including Porto Novo, Nagapattinam and Tranquebar, at the same time. It was believed that, in addition to the fact of the right-hand being less favoured, there were also problems because of the alteration in 'the Old Method of advancing Money on Contracts'.[18] The Europeans felt that the left-hand caste was more trustworthy and, in fact, the Dutch were reported to have 'turned off the right hand Cast, and used the left in their investments ...'.[19] As this aspect of the problem was not resolved, the disputes continued. The right-hand castes withdrew to San Thomé, and 'sent for the heads of their Cast out of the country ...'.[20] At this time the English made only minor concessions: they removed the boundary stones, and allowed exchange of houses until June 1708. In addition, it was made clear that the English were the masters in Madras, and neither Sa'adatullah Khan nor any of the other Mughal officials could do anything to change matters.

In effect, Black Town was divided between the two castes, with the left-hand caste being given the eastern side of the town, nearer the sea, and the right-hand being given the western side.[21] In 1717, it was decided that both castes were to be encouraged and 'kept in a Ballance, and neither suffer'd to claim a superiority over the other ...'.[22]

Settling caste disputes was only one aspect of the involvement of the British in Black Town. In numerical terms, the population of Black Town, from the beginning, outnumbered the handful of Europeans in White Town. But Fort St. George and its surroundings were always 'our Fort and town of Madraspatam', i.e. it was the Company that was held to be in charge. Undoubtedly, they needed Black Town's merchants, without whom they could not ply their trade; but the Black Town residents, during the seventeenth century, began to need them more. The balance had shifted: for the Company, trade was for profit; for the Indian merchants, trade from Madras was a matter of survival. The fact that the English accepted, and allowed, the traditional patterns in Black Town (as in the matter of separation along caste lines) made the adjustment easier; especially when profits were to be made, either directly in the Company's service or through the private trade of its factors. As mentioned earlier, the basis of the later *dubash* system, which was castigated so fiercely later, was laid at this time.

Black Town had its full complement of merchants, washers, bleachers, boatmen and others. The small English contingent at Fort St. George was more concerned with the security of the establishment than with maintaining day-to-day law and order in the town (unless, of course, it posed a threat to their security). They were, of course, very conscious of the freedom that the original grant had given them, of governing the town. They therefore actively resisted any attempts by Golconda, first, and the Mughals, later, to appoint an official (a *havaldar*) to look after the affairs of the town, and objected to any attempt to look outside Madras for redressal of grievances. This, in fact, was one of their main complaints against the Armenians, for they complained that, in case of any problem, the Armenians approached the Mughal officials directly, without reference to the English. Early in the eighteenth century, when numerous Muslims had settled at Madras, it was believed that most of them were spies of the government. The 'Persians and the Pattans' were also considered untrustworthy, and all the Muslims had grown 'very insolent'. They were ready 'to make applications to the Country Governors on all occasions'. The factors were therefore ordered to allow as few of them as possible, to settle in Madras, and if ever any justification was found, to drive out the others as well.[23] Ships belonging to the Mughals continued to put into Fort St. George and Fort St. David, and Daud Khan was also reported to have built a house at Mailapur, near San Thomé;[24] and, as far as possible, the factors tried to oblige the officials—but only if this could be done without jeopardizing their own position. For instance, they were prepared to give the Bakshi a bill of exchange for 'three hundred and sixty tomands to be paid in Persia'.[25] But they refused to surrender one of the merchants of Madras, who was reportedly in debt to Sa'adatullah Khan's brother at Vellore, for they feared the 'ill consequence' of giving up 'any inhabitants to the Justice of the Moors'.[26]

From the beginning, innumerable 'native functionaries' were associated with the Town. One very important functionary was the Peddanayak. The post of the Peddanayak was one that was familiar in the south, for, as head of the 'Talliars' (*talaiyaru*) or watchmen, he was responsible for maintaining the peace. The *talaiyaru* were probably the earliest form of police. In villages, they were concerned with petty thefts, and minor breaches of the peace, and offenders were probably arraigned before the panchayats (caste or village). In Black Town, the panchayat was replaced by the choultry court, but other than that, the functions remained the same. Payment was through an extra charge levied on all goods, called the 'Peddanague duty', which everyone, except Company officials, had to pay. In 1684, this duty was fixed at 'half a fanam per pagoda for Christians and three-quarters for others'.[27] Apparently, some attempts were made later to defraud the Peddanayak, for complaints were made that those liable to pay the Peddanayak duty were passing off their goods as belonging to the Europeans, who did not pay. Orders were therefore passed that if any European or Armenian was found allowing this, then the goods would be forfeited and 'He or they shall be fined at the pleasure of the Governour and Council'.[28] The Peddanayak was also in charge of maintaining the peace, and it was decided that all inhabitants would pay an annual duty of 'Three fanams for every great house, Two fanams for a smaller, and One fanam for the smallest of all'.[29] The earliest reference to the Peddanayak in the records comes from 1654, where the 'Peddy Nagues house and his free ground in the Village'[30] are mentioned. The area came to be known as Peddanaikpetta, a name it still retains.

In 1659, the terms of employment of the Peddanayak were worked out, and a *qaul* granted to Timappa (see Appendix III). He was to employ 50 peons, who would maintain peace in the town, and would therefore, be sent to any part of the town at the discretion of the Choultry court. They were to arrest any offenders, and would also be held responsible if anyone escaped and 'if any Merchant or Inhabitant of this Town shall run away, and any of your people, having knowledge thereof, shall conceal itt, that then you are to bring that party run away againe, and correct him that knew of his departure'.[31] In 1701 the number of peons was increased to 100. It was possible for the inhabitant of one town to take on the duties of the watch of another town, for Chinna Venkatadri was reported to have 'command of the watch of the towne' of Srikakulam.[32]

Apparently, the Peddanayak also had to pay a sum to the Golconda government, for there is mention of a sum of 200 pagodas which was 'formerly paid by the Peda Naigue once in 10 yeares'.[33] It was claimed that the Peddanayak of Pulicat paid 1,000 pagodas to the king, and Lingappa wanted the Peddanayak of Madras to pay the same amount, but later agreed to accept just the 200 pagodas. In 1688, it was decided to farm out the office to the highest bidder.[34]

Obviously, a similar system was in operation at Fort St. David as well. The appointment of peons or watchmen was left to the Peddanayak without too much interference by Company officials, and naturally, the tendency was to appoint people belonging to one village and one caste. The watchmen at Fort St. David were mainly from Udaiyarpalayam, which was also the place where both Fort St. George and Fort St. David merchants invested a great deal of money for the supply of cloth.[35] But while the English were prepared to accept these appointments, this too was only to a certain limit, for they refused to allow the Udaiyar of Udaiyarpalayam to nominate whomsoever he chose. The difference was that the Peddanayak was a functionary, who could be removed when necessary, but the Udaiyar was an independent local ruler whose involvement within the fort or settlement could not be tolerated.[36]

Another important functionary was the Conicoply (from the Tamil *Kanakkupillai*), who was in charge of maintaining the accounts at the Choultry. Most merchants employed their own Conicoplies, and in addition the English appointed a 'Town Conicoply', who was paid 20 pagodas per quarter. The post was passed on from father to son 'from the time of the

Jentue Kings through the Government of the King of Golconda the Moratas and the Mogulls …'. In 1696, the factors advised that the post be continued even if there were not too much work, for they said that 'if hee should be wholly ruined … he would … apply himselfe for satisfaction to the Nabob and Duan, where he would probably be heard … so far as to occasion us trouble …'.[37]

The Choultry was an important part of the administration of Madras. It was 'a court of petty causes, a custom-house, and a registration office for the record of sales of real property, and for the licensing of slaves'.[38] The Choultry began to function shortly after Fort St. George was established, and the first *adigar* (headman of the town) was Kanappa,[39] who occupied the position between 1644 and 1648. In 1648, it was decided to appoint Englishmen to act as magistrates at the Choultry. However, in 1661, the then Governor, Sir Edward Winter, decided to return to the old practice whereupon he appointed Timanna and Viranna to the Choultry. The next Governor reverted to the practice of appointing Englishmen, but decided that there would thenceforth be two Justices at the Choultry court.

In 1678 Streynsham Master reorganized the Choultry court. The number of justices was raised from two to three, and it was decided that at least two would be present during trials or registration of bills of sale of property. In order to make sure that the work was carried out properly, it was decided that the,

> … customer,[40] mintmaster (when there is one in that office), and Paymaster, or any two of them, do every Tuesday and Fryday sett in the Choultry to do the common Justice of the Towne as usuall, and do take care that the Scriven of the Choultry do duly Register all Sentences in Portuguez as formerly; and that there be an exact Register kept of all Alienations or sales of Slaves, houses, Gardens, boates, Shipps, etc…'.[41]

A brahman was usually appointed to the Choultry, at a salary of 177 *fanams* per month.[42]

All 'Rents and Revenues' were collected by the Customer, who was to maintain separate books for land and sea customs. Land customs included 'corne received for Toll in the paddy banksall … and also what received monthly for Company's part of the Weighers duty and for registering houses, slaves, etc.' Lists of land and sea customs received from Indians and Europeans, and lists of ships that put into or went out of Madras, together with point of origin or destination, were also be maintained.[43]

In 1680, it was decided to 'let to farme or Rent all the Choultry Customes that arises upon all Goods, Merchandize, Corne, Provisions and other things whatsoever which are not imported nor exported by sea for one whole yeare …'.[44]

In 1688, the duties to be paid on import and export of goods by land or sea from Madras, as well as anchorage duties for ships of varying tonnage, were laid down in detail.[45] All Englishmen whether Company servants or not, were to pay 4 per cent duty on the value of all goods imported or exported by sea. Jewels and bullion, which were the Company's monopoly, were exempted from this. Other Europeans were to pay 6 per cent. Goods laden at Madras, but not belonging to the Company, would pay half the custom duty, but nothing was charged on goods being re-exported. Land custom was also fixed at 4 per cent. If goods brought into Madras by a merchant were taken out again without being sold, then no further duty was to be paid; however, if they had been sold, then the buyer would have to pay 2 per cent duty.

Meanwhile, in 1678, it was decided to set up a Court of Judicature, because 'many complaints have lately been for want of a due course for the administration of justice'.[46] The Governor and Council were to meet every Wednesday and Saturday to hear cases, and their orders were to be executed by the Justices of the Choultry, and 'one Constable Bayly or Officer under them'. The idea of trial by a jury of 12 men was introduced in India at this time, and it was ordered that all court proceedings were to be taken down by a Clerk of the Court. The Choultry court would continue to handle 'all causes of small misdemeanour, matters of the peace, and actions of Debt of the sum of 50 pagodas New and under, … and also all other causes of a higher or greater vallue by consent of the partys, in all which cases (if any Partys find themselves agrieved) Appeales are or shall be allowed to the Court of the Governor & Councell …'.[47] In December 1678, it was decided to appoint a Clerk of the Market 'to prevent frauds and abuses in weights and measures, and to preserve good order in the Markets in the Towne and Suburbs'.[48] The weights and measures were to be stamped with the Company's seal, and any malpractices that were discovered to be decided at the Choultry court.

Between 1640 and 1680, the amount of land under the control of the Company was added to by the grant of numerous villages, including Egmore, Triplicane, and Nungambakkam (all part of present-day Chennai). In 1680, the Company managed to make a direct contract with the washermen to 'whiten, wash and beat the Company's cloth at more moderate rates then it hath been hitherto …'. The washers were to be paid directly by the Company, at specified rates (see Appendix II), so that they would have 'noe dependence upon any of the Companys Marchants or other whatsoever in this their business, but they shall be wholy under the Direction, protection and dependence of and upon ye Governour & Councell …'.[49] The part of the city occupied by the washers had, even earlier, been called Washermanpet; the contract made no difference, either to location or name. I have already discussed attempts to get weavers to settle near the town.

The population of Madras consisted of Telugu Beri Chettis, Tamil Komatis, Portuguese, Armenians, 'Moores', a few Frenchmen, and, of course, Englishmen, both free men and Company servants. The Portuguese who had moved to Madras from San Thomé shortly after the establishment of the fort were welcomed by the English, for it was believed that their presence would attract more Indians. In fact, in a petition of 1679, the Portuguese claimed that their presence drew 'Painters, Weavers, workemen and other inhabitants, who know only our command'.[50] As said earlier, the Portuguese were also important from the point of view of defence, for many of the soldiers of the fort were Portuguese. During the course of the century, however, the Portuguese came to be regarded much more warily, especially as they made frequent attempts to regain San Thomé. Orders were sent out that the Portuguese should not be allowed 'to settle quietly at St. Thoma', but 'such interruptions & molestations' were to be given 'as shall render that place too hot for them'.[51] Eventually the Portuguese did succeed in getting the grant of San Thomé from the Mughals, but by that time, the town had already become more or less what it is today, a suburb of Chennai. Many of the Portuguese continued to live at Black Town, for in 1706, when the Company was trying to recover the expense it had incurred in fortifying Black Town, the Portuguese were required to pay 3,300 pagodas, the highest sum.[52]

In 1687 a charter established a Mayor and Corporation for Madras, because 'the making and establishing of Corporations in Citties and Towns that are grown exceeding populous tends more to the well-governing of such populous Places, and the Increase of Trade, than the Constant use of the Law Martiall in trivial concerns ...'. The mayor was appointed for one year, and the new mayor was to be elected each year on 29 September from among the aldermen. There were to be twelve aldermen besides the mayor, of whom three were to be Englishmen, three Portuguese and seven 'Moores & Gentues'. The three Englishmen were to be Company servants, and if they left the Company's employ, they would not be aldermen any longer. In addition, it was stated that two brothers were not to be aldermen at the same time, and it was recommended that the factors 'so mix the heads of all Casts ... that you may alwayes hold the balance'.[53] There would be not more than 120 burgesses, who were to be elected by the mayor and aldermen. If an alderman's post fell vacant, it was to be filled by election from among the burgesses. A mayor's court was also established, which was empowered to try all civil or criminal cases, and was also a court of appeal in all civil cases where the 'value of the award exceeded 3 pagodas, and in criminal cases if the offender was sentenced to lose life or limb'.[54] In 1692, it was recommended that, for the future, most of the aldermen consist of 'the heads of severall forreigne Casts vizt. one or Two Hebrews, One or

Two Portugueze, and one or Two Gentues, and one Moore if you have a sufficient number of that Cast ...'.[55]

In 1678 suggestions were made about keeping the town clean 'after the Manner in England by taxing every house at a moderate rate, and to appoint a Scavinger to collect said monys, and therewith to hire Cooleys to carry away the dirt and filth...'. The 'Principall Persons' of the town objected to this, on the grounds that the 'Divan or the Mogull and Braminy Governors of the Country for the Kinge might come to know the great number of houses and familys that is in this Towne, and thereupon might raise new Impositions upon them and create trouble to the Towne ...'. According to the factors, the reality was that they were afraid that if such a list were made, then it would be easier for the English to tax them. In the same year, it was also suggested that quit rent be collected. However, as the practice was totally unfamiliar to the Indians, it was decided that the best way would be to 'make an absolute bargaine and sale of the grounds every purchaser paying for the purchase at a Reasonable rate to be set...'. All such purchases would be registered at the Choultry.[56]

Measures were taken for the maintenance of streets and houses in Black Town. It was decided that two persons 'dwellers in each Street, bee appointed by the Justices to bee Overseers thereof'. Their duty was to ensure that all due payments were properly collected, and that the streets were kept 'in repair and good order'. In addition, owners of houses in a dilapidated condition were given six months to 'decently repair, build or well fence the Same in, ... or Sell them to those that will'. Failing this, the Company would take over those houses 'to bee Sold or disposed of, as they shall think convenient'.[57]

Orders were also passed to safeguard the interests of the Indian merchants, whether those involved in Company trade or in private trade. No one in the Company's service was to be permitted to leave for England 'till he have paid all just debts to the Natives of India, or given bail to their actions'. In all cases, whether between Indians or between Indians and Englishmen, 'the Oaths of all native Indians of good fame & credit within the Agency of ffort St. George Shalbe admitted...'. In important cases, such oaths were to be repeated in the temples.[58] Other orders included the appointment of a *dubash*, who, unlike Timanna and Viranna, would not be involved in trade.

Constant efforts were made to attract merchants to settle at Madras. In 1688, an agreement was signed between the Armenians and the East India Company at London, giving the Armenians the right to trade to and from any of the ports to which the English traded, or where the English had a settlement, on the same terms that the English enjoyed.[59] The Armenians had begun to settle in Madras even earlier, for they were reported to have made Madras their permanent base on the Coromandel Coast from 1666.

They had been trading along the coast since the sixteenth century, and claimed to have directed the Portuguese to San Thomé.[60] Before long, the Armenians were reported to be among the richest inhabitants of Madras.[61] While there were not too many Armenians who lived permanently in Madras, there were many who traded from there, 'Yearly to Bengall, Manilha, Acheen, Persia, etc. or are Trading to the Kings Camp, Zulphaker Cawns Camp and Golcondah'. However, they declined to supply the Company with cloth, despite its offer of paying '15% on the prime cost'. While their stated reason was the unsettled state of the country, the factors maintained that in actual fact 15 per cent profit was far too little, 'when they expect twice or thrice as much profit by voyages'.[62] By the close of the century, a constant complaint was that the Armenians had taken over almost the entire trade of Madras, much to the detriment of the Company's trade.

In addition to the efforts made in Britain, the factors too were continually urged to increase the revenues of Madras by encouraging merchants to settle there and give them 'a free market and civill Treatment'.[63] Later, in the trade to China, the factors were advised to allow 'all others Inhabitants of our Fort & Town, whether they be English, Portuguez, or Natives' to join in the trade.[64] Private trade of the Company officials had already been permitted, 'to any Port or Places in the East Indies to the Northwards of the Equator, except Tonqueene and Formosa'.[65] At times, private trade was also regarded as necessary, as for instance, in the trade to Manila. Instructions were sent to develop this trade, 'But not under English names or as part of the Company as that would cause trouble with the Spanish rulers of the islands'.[66] The idea was to make Madras a 'Center of trade from all places of India wherein it is not convenient for us to establish Factories'. It was hoped that this would enable the factors to buy 'Pepper, China, Pegu & it may be in time, Nutmegs, Cloves, & many other Comodities, which otherwise you can never hope to purchase'.[67] Efforts to improve the revenues of Madras took many forms, including allowing merchants to take up farms. As has been mentioned earlier, the English managed to get the grant of several more villages near Madras, which were often farmed out to merchants. For example, in 1704, an individual 'Kittee Narain' was allowed to rent Egmore, 'Persiawaeke [Pursuvakkam] and Tandore' for seven years at 1,300 pagodas per annum. The factors also considered whether to take up farms for the Company, as, for example, of San Thomé. However, they were instructed not to do so unless they felt it was essential for the continued trade of Madras. It was finally decided that the Company's Indian merchants would rent it, for fear that the rent might be increased if it came to be known that the English were renting it.

Added to all this was the total freedom given in matters of religion. Black Town had an Armenian church, a mosque and several temples. The Court of Directors instructed the factors to 'allow to all their Natives the liberty of their Severall religions', and to make sure that no 'prejudice [was] done to Churches Mosques Pagodas or other Publick places where God is worshipped or pretended to be worshipped'.[68] It had been a custom of Black Town that the Muslims paid a small duty to the 'Gentue Pagodas', while the Hindus 'pay'd something to their Muskees [mosques]', but the payment by the Muslims had been discontinued since 1699. Following a petition by the Hindus, the Muslims were ordered to resume paying the duty.[69] While the English did not interfere in any matters concerning Indian religions, they remained concerned with the Christians. Marriages between Roman Catholics and Protestants were also permitted, mainly because the 'Roman Catholics of the Portuguez Nation' who had arrived with the establishment of Madras, were found to be 'Loyall and Serviceable in the defence of the place ... and our greatest income arises from the Customs upon their Commerce'.[70] However, they declared that all Englishmen were to be brought up as Protestants. No Portuguese priests were to be permitted to live in Madras, and the Roman Catholics were looked after by two French priests.

Throughout, the primary consideration for the English was always trade. Their treaties with the Indian princes, or the grants that they received from them, were directed as much towards freedom of trade in India, as security of trade in competition with the Dutch, and later, the French. The Dutch were far more strict in their dealings. In the seventeenth century, the Dutch came to be the real inheritors of the Portuguese system that had been superimposed on the Asian trading network. The Portuguese system had involved the building of fortresses at strategic places across Asia, and the issuing of passes to Asian shippers. Both the Dutch and the English continued the system of passes, but, while the English concentrated on India and her textiles, the Dutch tried to impose a monopoly of spices, through stricter control of Asian trade. No Asian trader was allowed to deal in cinnamon or pepper, as these were monopolies of the Dutch. After the India-Ceylon trade was taken over in the second half of the seventeenth century, areca nuts joined the list of articles that were a Dutch monopoly. Any vessel going east of Cape Comorin had to carry only a Dutch pass, for the passes of the other Europeans were not acceptable.[71] As a result the Dutch earned the hostility not only of the merchants, but also of the rulers, particularly of Malabar.

The Dutch attempts to increase their trade and income ranged from making their pagodas 'finer then the Standard of the Country',[72] to helping Golconda to besiege the French at San Thomé, to aiding the Thevar of Ramnad against the Nayak of Madurai (or vice versa, depending on what would bring them more profit). Far more than the English, they were prepared to use force to back up their demands.

The English certainly did admire some of the Dutch methods, for the factors were constantly urged to imitate the Dutch methods in raising revenues, so long as these did not put them into 'ye disaffeccion of ye People'.[73] They were also urged to do all they could to improve their position, for otherwise they would become so weak in India, that the Dutch would be able to 'rout them out of all India in one year, as they have already out of the noblest parts of India'.[74]

However, as mentioned earlier, in the long run, Dutch methods only served to arouse hostility. The question of religion also seems to have become a slightly problematic one for the Dutch. In the seventeenth century, Protestant fervour was still high in Europe, and particularly so among the Dutch, who, as Protestants, had won freedom from a Catholic country. Reformist zeal was at this time aimed more at Catholics than at non-Christian religions, but after the capture of Nagapattinam, when Dutch activities increasingly came to be concentrated along the Madurai/ Sri Lanka coasts, the Dutch came into contact with a primarily Catholic population. The Paravas, the inhabitants of this area, had been converted to Christianity by the Portuguese, and fiercely resisted Dutch attempts (led by Revd Baldaeus) to convert them to Protestantism. They were naturally more prepared to support local rulers (whether the Nayak of Thanjavur or Madurai, or the Thevar of Ramnad) and local merchants against the Dutch. On the other hand, the Dutch factors in India were in no position (even if they so desired), to enforce a religious agenda, for given the Portuguese networks (private traders and those of mixed Indian and Portuguese blood), such an emphasis would have been even more self-defeating.

The result was that the English were able to establish a more stable base in India. The monolithic, monopolistic organization of the Dutch East India Company, which depended on force, did not have any supporters, for they did not offer the Indian merchants any alternative to being wiped out of existence; the only choice was, whether to be destroyed by the (lack of) Indian political authority, or by the absolute Dutch commercial one. The English, on the other hand, first got the cooperation of the Indian merchants, and then used force.

But they did not succeed in attracting weavers and other artisans to the town. It was reported that during the famine, the Dutch had 'bought at Metchlepatam many of the prime workmen, Weavers, Painters etc. & transported them to their Colonyes',[75] and the English were criticized by the Court of Directors for not doing the same. In 1690, the then Governor, Elihu Yale, persuaded a few families of weavers to come and settle at Black Town, but that there were not too many weaver families even after that, is clear from Pitt's assessment of 1706, in which two castes of weavers were together liable to pay only 38 pagodas.[76] As mentioned earlier, it was only after 1730, when a suburb for weavers was established at Madras,

Chintadripetta, that the number of artisans in the town increased. By this time however, the English were steadily beginning to shift the scene of their operations to Bengal, so that the establishment of the weaver settlement did not have the same impact that it would have had some 50 years earlier. As it was, the English merely had the satisfaction of succeeding in fulfilling a long-held desire, at a time when it did not really to them much good. The focus was now on rivalry with the French, which manifested itself finally in the Anglo-French Wars.

Between famine (the coast was reported to be suffering from a series of famines in the early decades of the eighteenth century), increasing rivalry with the French, the emergence of the Arcot Nizamat, and the growing private trade, Fort St. George became more important in the political, and perhaps less so in the economic scheme of affairs of the Company.

Notes

1. It may be because of this earlier position as seat of government that even later, under Golconda rule, Poonamallee continued to be the seat of local government.
2. H.D. Love, ed., *Vestiges of Old Madras*, 3 vols., London, 1913 (henceforth *Vestiges*), vol. 1, p. 13.
3. Ibid., p. 40.
4. See Sanjay Subrahmanyam, *The Portuguese Empire in Asia, 1500–1700: A Political and Economic History*, London and New York: Longman, 1993, chaps. 7–9.
5. Records of Fort St. George, *Diary and Consultation Books* (henceforth RFSG, *Diary*), 31 May 1683.
6. RFSG, *Despatches from England, Letter to Fort St. George*, 16 March 1684.
7. Ibid., 6 January 1674.
8. Ibid., 20 September 1682.
9. Ibid., 16 March 1685.
10. RFSG, *Diary*, 3 January 1686.
11. The amount to be paid was 2 *fanams* per house.
12. RFSG, *Diary*, 29 February 1676.
13. Ibid., 3 and 4 January 1686.
14. *EFI*, n.s., vol. IV, p. 27.
15. RFSG, *Diary*, 26 June 1707.
16. Ibid., 17 July 1707.
17. Ibid., 26 August 1707.
18. RFSG, *Despatches to England*, 22 December 1707.
19. Ibid., *Abstract of Letter from Pitt to London*, 23 December 1707.
20. Ibid., 10 September 1707.
21. Even though the *idangai/valangai* division is no longer important, this division can still be seen in the older parts of Chennai.

22. *Vestiges*, vol. II, pp. 142–3.
23. RFSG, *Despatches from England, Letter to Fort St. George*, 2 February 1712.
24. S. Muhammad Husayn Nainar, tr. and ed., Burhan Ibn Hasan's *Tuzak-i-Walajah*, Madras, 1934, p. 64.
25. RFSG, *Diary*, 11 November 1702.
26. Ibid., 25 May 1713.
27. *Vestiges*, vol. I, p. 517.
28. RFSG, *Diary*, 10 May 1703.
29. Ibid., 24 December 1701.
30. *Vestiges*, vol. I, p. 417.
31. Ibid., vol. I, p. 419.
32. RFSG, *Diary*, 13 March 1679.
33. Ibid., 3 January 1679.
34. RFSG, *Despatches from England, Letter to Fort St. George*, 25 January 1688.
35. RFSG, *Fort St. David Consultations*, 20 December 1697.
36. Ibid., 12 December 1698. By 1698, most of the Poligars had become independent rulers, may be not of very large areas, but rulers nonetheless.
37. RFSG, *Despatches to England*, 6 March 1696.
38. *Vestiges*, vol. I, p. 126.
39. Ibid., p. 127. He apparently inherited this post from his father, who was said to have been in the Company's service from 1614.
40. The man in charge of collecting customs and the fourth in the Council at Fort St. George.
41. RFSG, *Diary*, 31 January 1678.
42. Ibid., 6 May 1678.
43. Ibid., 31 January 1678.
44. Ibid., 17 May 1680.
45. Ibid., 8 March 1688 and 5 April 1688.
46. Ibid., 18 March 1678.
47. Ibid.
48. Ibid., 9 December 1678.
49. RFSG, *Diary*, 13 May 1690.
50. Ibid., January 1679.
51. RFSG, *Despatches from England, Letter to Fort St. George*, 11 September 1689.
52. RFSG, *Diary*, 6 July 1706. The Company had earlier asked the inhabitants to work out an equitable distribution of the expense, but as they did not do so, the then Governor, Pitt, drew up an assessment. The Portuguese were assessed higher than the 'Chittee Cast' who were assessed at 2,000 pagodas.
53. RFSG, *Despatches from England, Letter to Fort St. George*, 28 September 1687.
54. *Vestiges*, vol. I, pp. 497–9.
55. RFSG, *Despatches from England, Letter to Fort St. George*, 22 January 1692.
56. RFSG, *Diary*, 16 December 1680.
57. Ibid., 9 July 1688.
58. RFSG, *Despatches from England*, 27 October 1682.

59. Ibid., 1688. The agreement was concluded on 22 June 1688.
60. Mesrovb Jacob Seth, *The Armenians in India from the Earliest Times to the Present Day: A Work of Original Research*, 1st pub Calcutta, 1937; rpt, New Delhi: Asian Educational Services, 1992, p. 579.
61. However, in Pitt's assessment, they would pay only 600 pagodas.
62. RFSG, *Despatches to England*, 6 March 1696.
63. RFSG, *Despatches from England*, 29 December 1680.
64. Ibid., 13 February 1684.
65. Ibid., 8 January 1674.
66. Ibid., 28 August 1682.
67. Ibid., 13 February 1684.
68. Ibid., 20 January 1685.
69. RFSG, *Diary*, 27 March 1707.
70. Ibid., 22 March 1680.
71. S. Arasaratnam, 'The Dutch East India Company and the Kingdom of Madura 1650–1700', *Tamil Culture*, vol. 12, 1963, pp. 70–1.
72. RFSG, *Despatches from England*, 8 January 1674.
73. Ibid., 20 July 1683.
74. Ibid., 14 January 1685.
75. RFSG, *Despatches from England*, 15 February 1689.
76. RFSG, *Diary*, 6 July 1706. The 'Kicull Warr Cast' was to pay 20 pagodas, and the 'Sallawarr Weavers' were to pay 18 pagodas.

CONCLUSION

'Running in the Same Place'

THE WHITE Queen said to Alice, in *Through the Looking Glass*: 'It takes all the running *you* can do, to keep in the same place. If you want to get somewhere else, you must run at least twice as fast as that!' This perhaps sums up the position of the Indian merchants at the end of our period. The structure to which they were acustomed had collapsed, but they were trying not to lose what they still had. So, their 'running' was an attempt to come up with a fresh set of equations, which would allow them to (at least) stay in the same place.

The Asian waters were the happy hunting ground of a great many people, and were, in manifold senses, contested terrain. Contests were necessarily at multiple levels, involving both the real and the ideological. Rights had to be won, maintained and asserted, and not necessarily in the same fashion. Access to existing rights and power equations were changing, and there was an urgent need to fit oneself into these emerging systems. Naturally, these equations included the relationship to the new polity. Wallerstein had seen the Indian Ocean area as either a world-economy or as a proto-world economy.[1] The world-systems theory is still a matter of considerable debate, for the nature of the Indian Ocean world and its own internal dynamics needs to be much better theorized. However, what is indisputable is the importance of India and the Indian Ocean world to the trade of the world.

At present there is much research on the importance of the Asian trade to capitalist accumulation in Europe, but the question of capitalism and its emergence within the Asian world remains one of the many 'what ifs?' of history. To go back to Wallerstein, he had identified four methods for the evolution of strong states, which were a prerequisite for the development of a world economy. These were bureaucratization, a monopoly on the use of force, the creation of legitimacy, in which all the elite participated, and the homogenization of the subject population. Excluding the last, it may be possible to argue that all these methods can be identified in seventeenth century India, particularly in the areas ruled by the Mughals, and so there was, as Frank Perlin has argued, some kind of 'proto-capitalism' or 'merchant capitalism'.[2] Such an application would lend credence to those theorists who argue that India had the potential, to which an abrupt end was put by the establishment of colonial rule.

On the other hand, most historians have also accepted that the Asian empires were primarily concerned with land rather than sea. That said, it is equally valid to point to the existence of an Indian Ocean littoral, with which the kings and princes were concerned at least from the point of view of customs duties. In the peninsula, naturally, the emphasis on such income was much greater—with the obvious corollary, that merchants and mercantile activity were much more the concern of the State than was the case in the more land-locked north.

Historically, merchants in south India, far from being on the periphery of the State, could be said to have had a definite and important role within it. This role was as important in the context of the smaller kingdoms that emerged in the course of the seventeenth and eighteenth centuries, as in the larger, older established kingdoms—whether Golconda, the Nayak kindgoms, or the kingoms of the Maravas. Rao, Shulman and Subrahmanyam have discussed in great detail[3] the activities of Citakkati Maraikkayar (Periya Tambi Maraikkayar) in the Ramnad kingdom. Somewhat similar, were the activities of Makhdum Nina at Fort St. David and Porto Novo. Merchants had contacts with the administration at all levels from the lowest to the highest, and often combined in themselves the roles of merchant and bureaucrat. The earlier discussion about Malaya, Chinanna and Mir Jumla makes it clear that they were able to use their dual roles to greatest effect. Their scale of activity obviously cannot be called a 'peddling trade'. On the other hand, that small-scale traders and exchanges were common in the port-to-port trade is also clear. The point I have been raising here, is not the scale of operations itself, but the way(s) in which such operations were affected (positively or negatively) by the politics of the interior.

The aspect of income from trade may not have been very important to kingdoms like Golconda as a whole (though even this is doubtful), but it is very clear that the governors, especially of Masulipattinam, found trade very lucrative.[4] I have already discussed the frequent complaints about the obstacles put in the way of their trade. One governor had farmed out the monopoly of changing money to a single *sarraf*. Later, there was also an attempt to restrict the English trade to certain specific merchants, so that the latter could, in effect, dictate the price of both sale and purchase to the former.[5] It is a different matter that the shift to Madras in 1640 did not help the English as much as they hoped, as before long, that part of the country had been conquered by Golconda. But even in this, it may be possible to infer that Golconda was loath to lose the income generated by English trade.

Many instances can be found of concessions made to increase trade. A *farman* regarding the settlement of a township in the Karnataka region said that the traders should be exempted from the *zakat* and other cesses in the newly settled area for a period of five years.[6] Both the *Golden Farman* and the grant for Madras referred to the importance of trade as a source of income. When Madras was besieged in 1657, the siege was raised in 1658 on the grounds that 'it was not profitable . . . to warr with merchants'.[7] Merchants were willing to come together against a common threat, as, for example, in a conflict between the Dutch and the Indians, when the latter made common cause with the English.[8] While the records are full of instances of obstacles to trade, no mention is made of the effect of such obstacles on Indian merchants. Keeping to the traditional theories would lead us to infer that the merchants were unaffected, for they were not concerned with State policies. On the other hand, it is also possible to argue that merchants were very concerned with wars, for, as suppliers, they stood to gain, no matter which side won. The latter, however, presupposes only brief periods of war, followed by stable political and economic systems once again; but this was definitely lacking in seventeenth-century south India.

Malaya, Chinanna and Mir Jumla were able to use force through the existing State structures to reinforce their position. But with Kasi Viranna, we find absolutely no mention of any kind of force. If any force was to be used, it had to come from the English Company, not from Viranna as an individual. His fortunes were totally bound up with Madras, in contrast to the earlier merchants, who ranged the length and breadth of the Coromandel, without limiting themselves to any one port.

Throughout the seventeenth century, the Dutch had always been willing to use force whenever and wherever required. The English 'progressed' from being told to appeal to the Indian rulers for help when necessary, to being told, at the end of the century, to use force when necessary, provided they had a 'fair excuse if afterwards questioned for it'. This was done in 1698. By 1706, the Court of Directors had begun to approve of action taken against the local rulers, which, they said, was the 'best way to make these treacherous People hearken to reason and prevent any future attempts on your Inhabitants ...'.[9] Equally approvingly, they remarked that the Dutch never 'missed any opportunity of raising, nor grudge at any pains in improving their revenues, those together with their Trade to and fro in the country and their spice and Jappan trade have . . . made them formidable to all the Powers round about their Settlements . . .' .[10] By 1711, however, the English were beginning to report that the Dutch investments had declined; and attempts made by the Dutch to borrow money from the Armenian merchants of Madras came to nothing.[11] What is significant is that from the 1680s, the English were increasingly talking of their 'martiall' power. The implication was that, to gain the stature of the Dutch, it was necessary to use force.

Early in the seventeenth century, the Portuguese had used their influence at the local courts to try to keep out the Dutch, but had not succeeded. The

Dutch then used their merchants to get concessions from the rulers, and later, when their merchants no longer had access to the courts, managed to force local rulers to sign treaties that gave them a monopoly. But the monopoly itself resulted in the decline of trade, and with the Dutch increasingly focusing their attention on Indonesia, their presence on the coast became virtually peripheral. It may be argued that they had marginalized themselves, by moving from Pulicat to Nagapattinam; but the move was in perfect accordance with the policies that they had consistently followed. They had moved to Pulicat in an attempt to get away from the control of Golconda; but when Pulicat also came within the Golconda Sultanate, they once again moved, this time to Nagapattinam, in the Nayak of Thanjavur's dominions. Also, their focus was always more on spices than on cloth, and control of the Bay of Madurai and the Sri Lanka coast was essential to their monopoly of pearls, chanks (conch shells), areca nuts and cinnamon in the far south. The English were well aware of the importance of the monopoly, for they declared that 'if ever they come to be Masters of yt commodity [pepper] as they are already of nutmegs, mace, cloves & Cinamon, the sole profitt of that one commodity will be more to them than all ye rest and in all probability sufficient to defray ye constant charge of a great Navy in Europe'.[12] The English did not really play any very important role in resisting the Dutch, but in the first two or three decades of the eighteenth century, Dutch investments in India began to decline. Still, they did continue to trade, both from the Coromandel Coast and from the Andhra coast. Early in the eighteenth century, they apparently decided to move further north of Masulipattinam, and applied for permission from the local Mughal *faujdar* to build a factory near Kakinada. The grant was made, but some problems with the local *zamindar* led them to settle at a small village, called Jagannaikpuram, which did offer some competition to the Masulipattinam trade.[13]

By the end of the seventeenth century itself, competition between the Dutch and the English began to be replaced by that between the French and the English. In some ways, events in the south can be seen as an extension of Portuguese activities one century earlier, i.e. they had used their influence at local courts to keep out their rivals, something that the English and the French now began to do. In the seventeenth century, the Portuguese had been unable to use force, as their power was already declining; but the English and the French, in the eighteenth century, were also prepared to use force. Even earlier, wars between nations in Europe had spilled over to India; now, when the local political situation had already resulted in postures of defence, such defensive measures could also be directed against other Europeans and the states in which they operated.

Thus, late in the eighteenth century (in 1787), Philip Francis, in his 'Speech on Indian Affairs' could, with complete justification, declare:

'From factories to forts, from forts to fortifications, from fortifications to garrisons, from garrisons to armies, the gradations were natural, and the result inevitable; where we could not find a danger, we were determined to find a quarrel.'[14] Clearly, even before colonial rule had been established, the modalities of acquiring power had been defined.

The main sufferers in all this were, naturally, the Indians, for it was their world that was visibly shrinking. The Europeans could retire behind their fort walls, or, in extreme cases, to their ships, to get away from their problems (the last was never resorted to, it just remained as a final option); but the Indians had no such options. Their fortunes were bound up with the local governments, and the fact that, when one local government fell, there was nothing comparable to replace it with, drove them ever nearer to the security offered by the Europeans. Given seventeenth century conditions, it is easy to see why Malaya, Chinanna and Mir Jumla had court connections, while Kasi Viranna had only local connections. By the middle of the century, the process of decentralization had taken firm hold, and so, Indian merchants were left with limited choices. They could move further south, to Jinji, Thanjavur or Madurai, or they could move nearer to the Europeans. Many did choose the former option, and until the 1680s, the records do, fairly frequently, mention that weavers, etc., had fled to the 'Chengy country' for shelter. This can also be seen as one reason for the success of Porto Novo, which had a large population of Indian merchants, who competed with the English at Fort St. David. If they stayed in Golconda, they may have (and did) suffer from the demands of the local administrators, but nonetheless that system also gave them room to manoeuvre.

The Mughal system was totally alien to the south Indian merchants, but given time, they would have adjusted to that as well. But the arrival of the Mughals, and the subsequent Mughal-Maratha conflict, also deprived them of the option of moving to Jinji. Moreover, there was no point in going farther south, as that would bring them within the purview of the monopolistic control of the Dutch. So, they were left with the choice of either the French or the English. The English had been on the coast for a longer period; more importantly, both at Madras and at Fort St. David they had set up a framework of legal institutions which incorporated some of the traditional institutions, and were also designed to promote trade. From the 1680s, the Court of Directors constantly issued instructions to the local factors about increasing revenue, and allowing merchants freedom of trade so long as the customs duties were paid. The English Company also allowed private trade, where, too, the Indian merchants had the opportunity to participate and make a profit. It is, therefore, not surprising that an increasing number of Indians began to draw closer to the English Company, in the pursiut of life, a reasonable amount of liberty, and profit. Only as English control increased, and as colonial rule took a firmer hold after the eighteenth century, did they lose the second, though the last was still possible, though on a reduced scale.

The Mughal conquest of the south after 1687 worsened rather than improved matters. For one thing, the functioning of the Mughal Empire was unfamiliar to the people of the south. More importantly, before any system could be brought in, the Mughal Empire had begun to disintegrate. Shortly after the conquest, the Deccan was divided into two *subas*, Hyderabad and the Karnataka. As mentioned earlier, the *faujdar* of the Karnataka was technically subordinate to the *subedar* of Hyderabad, but he reported directly to the Emperor. The result was to make the Emperor a very distant figure, in contrast to the situation under Golconda, where the Sultan was at Hyderabad. This naturally meant increased localization of power, a process which further heightened the tendency towards disintegration. In such a situation, alliance with one or the other of the Europeans was often the key to success. The Europeans, for their part, were primarily concerned with the continuation of trade and a steady supply of the products that their home markets required. Given the fact that most rulers ruled over a very small area, it was in the interest of the Europeans to try and acquire the entire hinterland under their control. This may be why the Anglo-French rivalry in trade spilled over into politics.

The policies followed by the British in the eighteenth century were based on their experiences with the situation vis-à-vis the Indian rulers, merchants, and their European competitors, and shaped by their own requirements. These requirements did include the paying of dividends to the shareholders back home in England, but also meant the building up of personal fortunes. In the quest for the latter, they managed to get the full support of the Indian merchants, and then to consolidate their hold, not just of their fort and factories, but of India as a whole.

In a rather different context (that of the Nayak kingdoms), it has been pointed out that the Nayaks had certain 'minimal components of statehood'.[15] These were money, mobility, a horizontal base, vertical linkages, and a deity or deities. With the possible exception of the last, it could be argued that all the Europeans, and, increasingly from our period, the English in particular, also had all this. Money they obviously brought in abundance—witness, not just the amounts invested by all the Companies on the coast, but also the money expended in what was euphemistically called 'presents' at the various courts. Mobility, too, was theirs, especially at sea. Just as the new Nayak elite had been willing to travel in search of fortune, so also the Europeans had travelled far, and were willing to engage in numerous activities for profit. Most of the Europeans—as corporates, not as individuals—did acquire a horizontal base, in the form of a port, which they fortified, and from where they could expand outwards. Given the fact that they had these three, vertical linkages could then be established with as many of the local powers as necessary, to continue their activities. The late eighteenth century title of 'Company Bahadur' can thus be viewed as one more in the series of efforts by the British to establish such linkages. Such efforts had begun at Masulipattinam and Surat, and had their fruition in grants like the *Golden Farman*, or the earlier grant from Sriranga, or the grant from Zulfiqar Khan and Daud Khan Panni. And finally, while there were no personal deities to give additional legitimacy, neither was there interference with the beliefs extant in the country either (at least, not by the English, and not in the period under review). Mention has been made of the temples in Madras, and of the decisions taken by the English in various matters concerning religion. At the same time, care was also taken to observe the customs of the country, as, for example, when a new *farman* was received at Fort St. George, the governor of the Fort and his council usually went to receive it outside the walls of the settlement. The *farman* was then carried in state through the town, accompanied by the sounds of 'trumpets drums and cymbals'. This kind of outward compliance would naturally lend emphasis to both, the vertical linkages, and the horizontal base.

Finally, the fluctuating conditions of the eighteenth century had led to the emergence of several smaller kingdoms, all of which were eager to get money, as well as control the sources of money. One obvious method of getting money was, of course, that the revenue that was collected was not remitted to the centre. Another method was to tap the foreigners. Unfortunately, the newly established kingdoms were, not surprisingly, less powerful than the old, and were unable to control the Companies. Contrary to their predecessors, these new kingdoms needed the support of the outside elements to maintain themselves, for they themselves were threatened by others who wished to share in the spoils. As the Europeans too needed to secure themselves and their investments, it was logical for them to try and control the new kings, and through them, their kingdoms. In the process, as mentioned earlier, Anglo-French rivalry was heightened. The rivalry that had begun with trade now extended to control over sources of the products used in that trade, and then to the land itself. Trade and politics thus entered a new phase, one in which the local rulers and merchants were pawns in the moves of the Companies.

In the course of the eighteenth century in particular, while the traditional contacts with the Indian Ocean littoral did not totally break down, it must be noted that control over, and access to, these contacts increasingly became filtered through the Europeans, and the English in particular. Thus, traditional markets may not have been totally lost to the Indian merchants, but they were definitely more limited, and there was no longer that direct contact which had existed earlier. Through the seventeenth century in south India and the eighteenth century in the rest of the peninsula, the merchants lost their access first to the political powers and structures that had supported them, and finally lost the structure itself, within which they had functioned. Though not reduced to the status of the 'comprador' merchant of Marx, yet they definitely did not have the range of activities of earlier days. Not surprisingly, subsequent references to Indian merchants are either as *dubashes* or as brokers, associated with the English Company or with the English in their capacity of private traders. A few instances remain of independent mercantile activity until about the 1760s, particularly from Porto Novo on the Coromandel Coast. However, even these began to decline with the loss of Manila to the British in the 1760s. Thereafter, the Industrial Revolution and the establishment of colonial rule completed the process begun in the seventeenth century.

There is no denying that all merchants had to live and work with the reality of the gradual loss of their traditional domains throughout the period under review. When to this was added the occasional natural disaster, the operations of these merchants were further affected, as happened in the south in the early eighteenth century. The merchants did recover, and very well, from the Gujarat famine of the 1630s, as can be seen from the fact that merchants like Virji Vora and Abdul Ghafur seem to have built up their networks only after that event. However, it is difficult to ascertain how much of this recovery was due to an impetus given by the State. It is clear that the State was directly involved in the process of recovering from the famine, for there are references to loans being given to the peasants, and to reductions in the amount of revenue to be paid by them. Such actions would have benefited, at least indirectly, the merchants as well.

Recovery from man-made crises was rather more difficult. On the west coast, Surat was undoubtedly affected by Shivaji's raids, while the abandonment of Rajapur could also be laid at his door. It is undoubtedly true that part of the reason for Shivaji's actions in Rajapur was his need to enforce greater control over the Europeans, and so, when the English proved unwilling to fall in line, he offered the place to the French—perhaps in the hope that provoking competition would help his own people to benefit. On the other hand, it is equally true that his raid on Surat exposed the inability of the Empire to defend itself and its subjects. Thus, defence increasingly became a local need, to be locally met. It can be argued that the ability of the Dutch and the English to defend themselves against Shivaji drew more Indians towards them, and, in fact, the records for the period after the 1660s for both the coasts make frequent mention of the influx of people because of the 'security' that the English settlements offered. Perhaps no greater proof of this can be found than in the fact that, early in the eighteenth century Daud Khan Panni, the Mughal general in the south, sent his family to his house in Madras for their safety (he had earlier purchased a house there).

On the other hand, it is necessary to examine the actual nature of this security. Were these forts/enclaves really secure? For much of the seventeenth century, despite problems on the Indian political scene, the answer would have to be 'no'. It should be remembered that while war was (and is) often dictated by hopes of both political and economic gain, warfare is also an expensive business. During the seventeenth century, the Europeans may have provided the most visible and the most vulnerable targets, precisely because they were outsiders, and therefore lacked the access or manoeuvrability that Indian merchants possessed. However, during the seventeenth century, and even more in the eighteenth century, as the political systems declined, it was this access that was lost. It is noticeable that the records make more frequent mention of migration. But, where earlier such migration was to areas having a more familiar system—to the Jinji country in the case of the Coromandel region, away from Golconda and Bijapur, and to the Maratha or Mughal regions in the case of the Konkan—in later periods, it was to the European enclaves. The French settlement at Pondicherri got a large number of weavers when the Mughals besieged Jinji, and later as well, when the Arcot Nawabi was being set up. Similarly, the English at Bombay benefited considerably when the Mughal-Maratha conflict was at its height. Given the greater degree of warfare in the Deccan from the 1660s, artisans, in particular, seem to have sought the only areas where they could be relatively free. As stated earlier, security of life and occupation were increasingly seen to be available only from those not directly involved in the political manoeuvrings then going on, i.e. the English, and later the French. In this, the Dutch and the Portuguese do not seem to have provided a viable alternative, as both were seen as being too restrictive. The monopolistic practices adopted by the Portuguese first and the Dutch later made the (relative) freedom of the English and French settlements more attractive. It is a fact that both the English and the French placed no major restrictions on trade to and from their settlements, which remained part of the country trade network, especially on the Coromandel Coast.

The seventeenth century was the period of individual traders like Malaya Chetti or Kasi Viranna on the Coromandel Coast and Virji Vora and Abdul Ghafur on the west coast; of merchants in politics, like Malaya Chetti and Mir Jumla on the east coast, but none of the same kind on the west; and finally, of merchants and East India Companies, like Kasi Viranna and Ananda Ranga Pillai on the east coast, and families like the Rustumjis and the Parekhs on the west coast. The eighteenth century was one where many, including Indian merchants like Abdul Ghafur's grandson, jockeyed for position, but failed. In the period under review, it cannot be said that the English, at least were beginning to emerge as the supreme power, for control by local political powers continued to be exercised—firmly, on the west coast, as in the case of Kanhoji, and rather less so, in the case of Sa'adatullah Khan of Arcot.

If one is to argue that the pre-modern eras did consist of different worlds and that these worlds consisted of the ritual or the ideological, the political and the economic, then the modern would have to be identified as that in which the ritual acquired formal overtones, but it was the political as the public that finally became the sphere of importance. The ritual provided the formal framework of action, for, it included religion and tradition and therefore assigned status and roles. One part of this status was undoubtedly caste. But at another level, it must be remembered that caste was also a label of identity and was far from being the unchanging structure beloved of later colonial writings. Therefore, political or economic status could also be accommodated within a ritual setup. In south India, such a setup was provided by the left-hand/right-hand division. The use of the temple to create a sacred landscape, but one that was defined by a political and ideological authority can be seen as yet another dimension of this accommodation.

It may be argued that, one of the crucial changes of the seventeenth century was the loss of a certain ideological and political framework within which patterns of assimilation and accommodation could be adjusted. The loss of political structures of legitimation left the merchants in particular with only an economic identity, which too began to be eroded. Given the close connections between the fortunes of the merchants and the states which supported them, the loss of one would soon affect the other. The narrowing of the political world meant, at the same time, a need to depend more on the economic and social world (which would also mean a greater emphasis on caste, and may explain to some extent the caste conflicts of the seventeenth and eighteenth centuries), and also a search for alternatives. The older forms now began to be replaced with one in which there was a closer connection between the political and the economic, bypassing the ideological, or rather, substituting a newer ideology—that of the emerging colonial world. In this, the polity was that of the mother country, and the local economies were subsumed to the requirements of that economy.

Only those who were able to straddle both the worlds—of the new polity and the emerging world economy—could then survive. It is in this light, therefore, that one may need to re-examine the role of Armenian merchants in the eighteenth century. By the terms of a treaty signed in London in 1688, the Armenians had been given the right to trade on the same terms as the English East India Company from all the places where the Company had a trading settlement. With their old-established networks all over the Asian trading world, and the new concessions that they now got, they became one of the most important trading groups, rivalling the Europeans and competing with them on equal terms. But their hold was on economy alone, and on the networks established through their trade. Access to the political world was neither sought nor required. Through the seventeenth century, the nature of the links between trade and politics had been re-worked, and in the eighteenth century, these links acquired new forms. The older political frameworks, which had supported the Indian merchants and been supported by them gradually disappeared, to be replaced by a new structure, which linked the Indian economy to the colonial polity, then re-shaped that economy totally.

The eighteenth century witnessed attempts to create new solutions to changed equations. These attempts included Kanhoji Angré's efforts to establish at least a limited sovereignty at sea, Martanda Varma's much more successful establishing of a pepper empire and the abortive moves of Sa'adatullah Khan to draw Indian traders to his new port. The Armenians were another dimension of the same efforts, for they had trade without any political connections or bases—in other words, they functioned comfortably in a world in which polity and economy were delinked. The English and the French sought to reconnect the two on their own terms; and so they competed over access to production areas in the arena of polity. The establishment of the British Colonial Empire completed the process that had begun in the seventeenth century to give the empire a new form and direction in which the older world was reduced, if it existed at all, to a shadow of its former self and without a 'world' in which to function.

The ability to use force and the ability to manoeuvre political systems, either through the direct use of force, or a combination of conciliation and coercion, passed, in the course of the period under review, out of the realm of possibility of the Indian merchant, and into the hands of the Europeans. In the course of the eighteenth century it passed entirely into the hands of the British, to make both trade and politics their domain, to be distributed, shared, or delegated as per their choices and requirements.

Notes

1. Immanuel Wallerstein, *The Modern World System: Capitalist Agriculture and the Origins of the European World-Economy in the Sixteenth Century*, New York: Academic Press, 1974, p. 331.
2. Frank Perlin, 'Proto-Industrialization and Pre-Colonial South Asia', *Past and Present*, vol. 98, 1983, pp. 30–95.
3. V. Narayan Rao, D. Shulman and Sanjay Subrahmanyam, *Symbols of Substance: Court and State in Nayaka Period Tamilnadu*, Delhi: Oxford University Press, 1998, chap. VII, pp. 264–304.
4. One indication is that the annual farm of Masulipattinam was 1,80,000 pagodas. See H.K. Sherwani, 'Administration, International Conduct and Social Conditions under Abdullah Qutb Shah', *Journal of Indian History*, 1966, p. 11.
5. W. Foster, ed., *The English Factories in India* (henceforth *EFI*), Oxford: Clarendon Press, 1906–27, n.s., ed. C. Fawcett, 4 vols., 1624–9, p. 282.

6. Y.H. Khan, ed., *Farmans and Sanads of the Deccan Sultans*, Hyderabad, 1963, p. 14.
7. *EFI*, 1655–60, p. 175.
8. Ibid., 1665–67, pp. 242–3.
9. Records of Fort St. George (henceforth RFSG), *Despatches from England*, 18 January 1706.
10. Ibid., 4 February 1708.
11. RFSG, *Despatches to England, Fort St. George to Company*, 11 January 1713.
12. RFSG, *Despatches from England, Letter to Bombay*, 3 August 1687.
13. S. Arasaratnam and A. Ray, *Masulipatam and Cambay: A History of Two Port Towns, 1500–1800*, Delhi: Munshiram Manoharlal, 1994, p. 96.
14. Quoted by W. Hickey, *Tanjore Maratta Principality in South India*, Madras: C. Foster & Co., 1872, p. 124.
15. Rao, Shulman and Subrahmanyam, *Symbols of Substance*, op. cit., pp. 54–5.

Appendix I

List of castes included in left- and right-hand divisions according to F. Buchanan

'The tribes, or castes, comprehended in the Eddagai, or left hand side, are nine.

(1) Panchala, comprehending,
  (i) The Cubbinadeva, or blacksmiths,
  (ii) Badiga, carpenters,
  (iii) Cunsugaru, coppersmiths,
  (iv) Cul'badiga, masons, and
  (v) Axala, gold and silversmiths.
(2) Bheri Chetty, merchants, who pretend to be of the Vaisya caste.
(3) Devanga, a class of weavers.
(4) Haganigaru, oilmakers, who use 2 oxen in their mills.
(5) Gollur, or Golawarlu, who transport money.
(6) Paliwanlu (a tribe of cultivators, who are not of Karnataca origin).
(7) Palawanlu (a tribe of cultivators).
(8) Baydaru, hunters.
(9) Madigaru, tanners or shoemakers. The Panchala command the whole party. ...'

'The castes forming the Ballagai, or right hand side, are 18 in number.

(1) Banijigaru, who are of many trades, and many religions. The two most conspicuous divisions are:
  (1) Panchum Banijigaru, who are traders and wear the Linga.
  (2) Teliga Banijigaru, who worhip Vishnu.
(2) Wochgaru, cultivators of the Sudra caste, and of Karnataca extraction.
(3) Jotiphana, oilmakers, who use one bullock in the mill.
(4) Rungaru, calico printers, and taylors.
(5) Ladarau, a kind of Mussulman traders, who are followed by all the artificers of the same religion.
(6) Gujerati, merchants of Gujerat.
(7) Camatigaru, persons who are really of the Vaisya caste.
(8) Jainaru, worshippers of Jain.
(9) Curubaru, shepherds, blanket-weavers, and cultivators.
(10) Cumbaru, potters.
(11) Agasaru, washermen.
(12) Besta, palankeen-bearers.

(13) Padma Shalayvaru, a kind of weavers.
(14) Naindaru, barbers.
(15) Uparu, persons who dig tanks, and build rough walls.
(16) Chitragaru, painters.
(17) Goallaru, keepers of cows and buffaloes.
(18) Whalliaru. The people called Parriars at Madras....'

The Panchum Banijigaru are the leaders of this division.

Source: Francis Buchanan, *A Journey from Madras through the Countries of Mysore, Canara and Malabar in the year 1800*, London: Cadell and Davies, 1807, pp. 77–8.

Appendix II

Increase in rates sought by washers: 2 April 1706

Specified cloth	*Existing rates*	*Increase sought*	*Total*
Long cloth	36 *fanams/corge*†	2 *doodas**/piece	41 *fanams (f)/corge (c)*
Salampores	16 *fanams/corge*	1 *dooda*/piece	18 *f* 40 *c* 20 *coveds*+/*corge*
Morees	10 *fanams/corge*	1 *dooda*/piece	12 *f* 40 *c* 40 *coveds*/*corge*
Ginghams	32 *fanams/corge*	3 *doodas*/piece	39 *f* 40 *c* /*corge*
Fine Morees	12 *fanams*/piece	1 *dooda*/piece	14 *f* 40 *c* /piece
Neck Cloth	5 *doodas*/piece	3 *cash*/piece	1 *f* / 16 *coveds*
Fine Gingham	10 *fanams/corge*	1 *dooda*/piece	12 *f* 40 *c* /*corge*

Notes: * This is the only time that this word appears in the records, and the currency equivalent is not clear.

+ A *coved* is a measure of cloth (18 inches).

† A *corge* refers to a set of twenty pieces of cloth.

Source: RFSG, *Diary*, 2 April 1706.

Appendix III

'Copy of Cowle given to Pedda Nague [by Chambers in 1659], entered in Diary of 1686

'Whereas formerly you watched out Towne with 20 Peons, & having not sufficient maintenance allowed to contest you, for 2 or 3 years you left that Imployment, Saying also that 20 Peons, the Town being greater than formerly were not sufficient to watch itt, wherefore we made this agreement with you as followeth Vizt.

'That Moorte Nagues Son Timmapa, shall build a house & dwell in the Towne, & watch the Said Town, with 50 Peons, and for the Said Service you shall be allowed the following duties Vizt.

'That you shall have 18 Paddy fields given you rent free.

'That out of every Stack of Paddy you shall have one Bundle in the Ear, and one Tombe grain.

'That out of what graine Soever growes within the bounds of the Towne, you shall be allowed 6 measures out of every Collome.

'That the Fisher men shall pay you per Ann 225 fanams.

'That those that buy Fish, & carry it out of Towne, shall pay out of every fanams worth 4^{ca}.

'That out of every draught of Fish you shall be allowed 10 Fish.

'That for Fishing in the River shall be allowd you 10^{fa} per Annum.

'That for what goods is brought in the Choultry the Company receives^{fa} 1.36^{ca} out of every Pagoda for Custome, & formerly was allowed you 12^{ca} per Pagoda, now shall be given you 16^{ca} per Pagoda.

'That for what Paddy & Rice shall be brought into the Town on Oxen, that out of every great bagg, Shall be allowed you $^3/_4$ of a Small measure, & out of every Small bagg $^1/_2$ a Small measure.

'That out of every Small bagg, Rice or Paddy that shall bee brought by any Cooley into the Town, you shall be allowed $^1/_6$ part of a Small measure.

'That the Oyle men shall allow you every time they fill their Mill $^1/_6$ part of a Small measure of Oyle.

'That out of every 20000 Bettle Nuts you shall be allowed 30.

'That out every Maund Pepper you shall be allowed 4 [?].

'That out of every Shop that sells Betle shall be allowed you dayly 1 Bettle Nut 3 Leaves 1 Bunco Tobacco.

'That every Vessell that arrives shall allow you 5 fanams.

'That every Boat laden with Wood shall allow you 2 fans.

'That whereas formerly was allowed you 4^{ca} per Pag^{o} for Custome of Cloth, that now shall be allowed you for all Sorts of Goods, brought into the Town, or carried out of Town, 6^{ca} per Pag^{o} the Compas. goods excepted.

'That all the Inhabitants of the Town, excepting Christians, & the old Servants belonging to the Compa. shall pay you per Ann 3 fanams for every great house, 2[fa] for a Smaler, & 1[fa] for the Smallest of all.

'But for what Rice or Paddy shall be delivered by us to any Merchant you are not to receive any Custome, for that, According to which agreement we give you this our Cowle, Also that the 50 Peons aforesaid, Shall be imployed about the Town, as he that hath the charge of the Choultree, shall think fitting, And if any man shall be delivered by us into your Custody, and shall make his escape, that you Shall pay the debt, the person escaped owed. Also that if we should go abroad att any time, to take our pleasure, you shall procure 100 or 150 Peons to accompany us. And if occation shall require 150 or 200 Peons, your Timmapa, with the Said Peons shall go, upon what imployment we shall send him, & also allow them 4 dayes batty, but if we Should detain them longer, that then we are to give them batty, Also if any House is robbed, that you shall make satisfaction for what is lost, And if any Merchant or Inhabitant of this Towne shall run away, and any of your people having knowledge thereof, shall conceal itt, that then you are to bring that party run away againe, & correct him that knew of his departure....'

Notes: [ca] = cash; [fa] = fanam(s) and Pag[o] = Pagodas
Source: RFSG, *Diary,* 1686.

Appendix IV

Custom Rates and Prices

TABLE IV.1: Comparative Land Customs Rates, 1711 and 1720

Heads	*1711*						*1720*					
	February			*June*			*February*			*June*		
	P	*F*	*C*	*P*	*F*	*C*	*P*	*F*	*C*	*P*	*F*	*C*
Choultry custom	165	4	36	339	27	36	240	32	57	563	16	62
Ruby brokers	2	10	55	102	12	25	9	14	14	51	13	67
Registering slaves	1	4	–	1	12	–	2	16	–	4	–	–
TOTAL	168	18	91	442	51	61	251	62	71	617*	29	129

TABLE IV.2: Comparative Sea Customs Rates, 1711 and 1720

Heads	*1711*						*1720*					
	February			*June*			*February*			*June*		
	P	*F*	*C*	*P*	*F*	*C*	*P*	*F*	*C*	*P*	*F*	*C*
Goods imported and exported	640	35	28	2952	27	72	416	12	42	2392	34	28
Grain	48	5	24	187	35	0	–	–	–	1234	2	52
Anchorage	3	0	0	40	0	0	5	0	0	31	18	0
TOTAL	691	40	52	3718*	62	72	421	12	42	3708*	54	80

Notes: *P* = Pagoda, *F* = Fanam, *C* = Cash. 1 Pagoda = 36 Fanam, 1 Fanam = 80 Cash.
* Mistake in the Records, the totals should actually be 618, 3179 and 3657 respectively.
Source: RFSG, *Diary*, 1711 and 1720.

TABLE IV.3: Prices of Textiles, 1688–1701

Name of textile	*Year*	*Measurement*		*Number of pieces required*	*Price (per corge of 20 pieces)*		
		*Coved**	*Coved*		*P*	*F*	*C*
Longcloth (ordinary)	1688	–	–	–	22	–	–
	1699	72 long	2 1/4 broad	15,000	34	–	–
	1700	72 long	2 1/4 broad	30,000	34	–	–
	1701	72 long	2 1/4 broad	20,000	36	1	–
Salempores (ordinary)	1688	–	–	–	10	25	–
	1699	32 long	2 1/8 broad	10,000	16	18	–
	1700	32 long	2 1/8 broad	4,000	29	–	–
	1701	32 long	2 1/3 broad	4,000	30	26	–
Morees (ordinary)	1688	–	–	–	–	–	–
	1699	20 long	2 1/2 broad	8,000	20	–	–
	1700	–	–	–	–	–	–
	1701	–	–	–	–	–	–
'Betellas oringal' (Warangal)	1688	–	–	–	–	–	–
	1699	32 long	2 broad	5,000	70	–	–
	1700	32 long	2 broad	6,000	70	–	–
	1701	32 long	2 broad	7,000	74	7	–
Gingham	1688	16 long	2 broad	–	23	–	–
	1699	16 long	1 7/8 broad	1,000	32	–	–
	1700	–	–	–	–	–	–
	1701	–	–	–	–	–	–

Note: * A *coved* is a measure of cloth (18 inches).
Source: RFSG, *Diary*, 6 September 1688, 14 April 1688, 16 August 1700 and 11 November 1701.

TABLE IV.4: European Goods delivered to Indian Merchants for Contract, September 1688

Specifications	*Pieces*	*Price in pagodas*
Broadcloth (fine)	12	@ 52 per ½ piece
Aurora	48	@ 52 per ½ piece
Broadcloth (ordinary)	120	@ 22 per ½ piece
Perpetuanoes (fine)	50	@ 12 per piece
Perpetuanoes (ordinary)	250	@ 7 per piece
Lead for candyes	–	Paid for in pagodas 10 per candy
Silver	–	£17 : 1/4 per 10 pagodas

Source: RFSG, *Diary*, 6 September 1688.

Bibliography

Primary Sources

Records of Fort St. George, *Diary and Consultation Books*.
Records of Fort St. George, *Despatches to England*.
Records of Fort St. George, *Despatches from England*.
Records of Fort St. George, *Letters from Fort St. George to Subordinate Factories*.
Records of Fort St. George, *Letters from Subordinate Factories to Fort St. George*.
Records of Fort St. George, *Fort St. David Consultations*.
Minutes of Proceedings in the Mayor's Court of Madraspatam, June-December 1689, July 1716–March 1719.
Selections from the Dutch Records:
(A) *Record of Dutch Commercial Treaties in India*, 1567–1688 (in English).
(B) *Dutch Treaties*, 1643–1711 (in English).

Published Sources

Annual Reports on South Indian Epigraphy, Archaeological Survey of India, 1987.
Census of the Madras Presidency, 1871, Madras Records Office, Madras.
Correspondence Relating to the Settlement of Ramnad and Sivaganga Zamindaries, Madras Records Office, Madras.
Papers Relating to the History of Cumbum, Cudalore and Pudupatty, Madras Records Office, Madras.
Statistical Atlas of the Madras Presidency, Madras Records Office, Madras, 1895.
Subrahmanya Aiyer, K.V., ed., *South Indian Inscriptions*, Archaeological Survey of India, New Delhi.
Subramaniam, T., ed., *South Indian Temple Inscriptions*, 3 vol., Madras, 1957.

Persian Sources (Translated)

Elliot and Dowson, *History of India as told by its own Historians*, 8 vol., London, 1867–77.
Haig, T. Wolseley and K. Ahmed, eds., Khafi Khan's *Muntakhab-ul-Lubab*, 2 vols., Calcutta: Bib. Ind., 1869.
Khobrekar, V.G., ed., *Sir Jadunath Sarkar Birth Centenary Commemoration Volume*: English Translation of Bhimsen's *Tarikh-i-Dilkusha* (Memoirs of Bhimsen Relating to Aurangzeb's Deccan Campaign), Bombay: Department of Archives, Maharashtra, 1972.
Nainar, S. Muhammad Husayn, tr. and ed., Burhan Ibn Hasan's *Tuzak-i-Walajah*, Madras: University of Madras, 1934.

Sarkar, Jadunath, tr. and ed., Saqi Musta'id Khan's *Ma'asir-i-Alamgiri,* Calcutta: Royal Asiatic Society of Bengal, 1947.

Traveller's Accounts/Diaries

Buchanan, F., *A Journey from Madras through the Countries of Mysore, Canara and Malabar in the year 1800*, London: Cadell and Davies, 1807.

Crooke, W., ed., John Fryer's *A New Account of East India and Persia, Being Nine Years' Travel 1672–1681*, London: Hakluyt Society, second series, 1909; New Delhi: Asian Educational Services, rpt, 1996.

Crooke, W. and V. Ball, Jean-Baptiste Tavernier's *Travels in India*, 2 vols., Indian edn, Delhi: Munshiram Manoharlal, 1977.

Dames, M.L., tr. and ed., *The Book of Duarte Barbosa*, 2 vols., London: Hakluyt Society, 1918.

Lady Fawcett, tr. and Charles Fawcett, ed., *The Travels of the Abbé Carré in India and the Near East, 1672–1674*, London: Hakluyt Society, 1948; New Delhi: Asian Educational Services, rpt, 1990.

Irvine, W., tr. and ed., *Manucci's Storia do Mogor, or Mughal India,* 4 vols., London: John Murray, 1907–8.

Moreland, W.H., *The Voyage of Peter Floris,* London: Hakluyt Society, 1934.

———, ed., *Relations of Golconda in the Seventeenth Century*, London: Hakluyt Society, 1931.

Price, J.F. and K. Rangachari, eds., *The Private Diary of Ananda Ranga Pillai, Dubash to Joseph Francois Dupleix, Governor of Pondicherry*, 12 vols., Madras: Government Press, 1904–28.

Smith, V.A., tr. and ed., *Francois Bernier's Travels in the Mogul Empire*, London: Oxford University Press, 1934, Indian edn, New Delhi: Munshiram Manoharlal, 1983.

Temple, R.C., ed., Thomas Bowrey's *A Geographical Account of the Countries Around the Bay of Bengal 1669–1679*, London: Hakluyt Society, 1905; Indian edn, New Delhi: Munshiram Manoharlal, 1997.

———, ed., *The Diaries of Streynsham Master*, 2 vols., London: Published for the Government of India, 1911.

Varadarajan, Lotika, tr. and ed., *India of the 17th Century: Memoirs of Francois Martin (1670–1694)*, 4 vols., New Delhi: Manohar, 1981–4.

Yule, H. and R. Barlow, ed., *The Diary of William Hedges*, London: Hakluyt Society, 1886–8.

Secondary Sources

Books

Abraham, M.M., *Two Medieval Merchant Guilds of South India*, New Delhi: Manohar, 1988.

Aiyar, Sathianatha, R., *History of the Nayaks of Madura*, Oxford: Oxford University Press, 1924; New Delhi: Asian Educational Services, rpt, 1991.

Appadorai, A., *Economic Conditions in Southern India, AD 1000–1500*, 2 vols., Madras: University of Madras, 1936.

Arasaratnam, S., *Merchants, Companies and Commerce on the Coromandel Coast, 1650–1750*, Delhi: Oxford University Press, 1986.

_______, *Maritime India in the Seventeenth Century*, Delhi: Oxford University Press, 1994.

_______, *Maritime Commerce and English Power: Southeast India, 1750–1800*, New Delhi: Sterling Publishers, 1996.

Arokiaswami, M., *The Kongu Country*, Madras: Madras University Press, 1956.

Balkrishna, *Commercial Relations between India and England, 1601–1757*, London: G. Routledge & Sons, 1924.

Banga, Indu, ed., *Ports and their Hinterlands in India, 1700–1950*, New Delhi: Manohar, 1992.

Bayly, S., *Saints, Goddesses and Kings: Muslims and Christians in South Indian Society, 1700–1900*, Cambridge: Cambridge University Press, 2004.

Bouchon, Genevieve, *'Regent of the Sea': Cannanore's Response to Portuguese Expansion, 1507–1528*, tr. Louise Shackley, Delhi: Oxford University Press, 1988.

Boxer, C.R., *The Dutch Seaborne Empire*, London: Hutchinson, 1965.

Champakalakshmi, R., *Trade, Ideology and Urbanisation*, Delhi: Oxford University Press, 1996.

Chicherov, A.I., *Indian Economic Development in the 16th to 18th Centuries*, Moscow, 1965; revised edn, 1998; Indian edn, New Delhi: Manohar, 1998.

Chaudhuri, K.N., *The Trading World of Asia and the English East India Company, 1660–1760*, Cambridge: Cambridge University Press, 1978.

_______, *Trade and Civilisation in the Indian Ocean: An Economic History from the Rise of Islam to 1750*, Cambridge: Cambridge University Press, 1985.

Chaudhury, S., *Trade and Commercial Organisation in Bengal, 1650–1720*, Calcutta: Firma K.L. Mukhopadhyay, 1975.

_______ and M. Morineau, eds., *Merchants, Companies and Trade: Europe and Asia in the Early Modern Era*, Cambridge: Cambridge University Press, 1999.

Curtin, P., *Cross-Cultural Trade in World History*, Cambridge: Cambridge University Press, 1984.

Danvers, F.C. and W. Foster, eds., *Letters Received by the East India Company from its Servants in the East*, 6 vols., London, 1896–1902.

Das Gupta, A., *Malabar in Asian Trade 1740–1800*, Cambridge: Cambridge University Press, 1967.

_______, *Indian Merchants and the Decline of Surat 1700–1740*, Wiesbaden, 1979; New Delhi: Manohar, rpt, 1994.

Das Gupta, A. and M.N. Pearson, eds., *India and the Indian Ocean, 1500–1800*, Calcutta: Oxford University Press, 1987.

Fawcett, C., ed., *The East Coast and Bengal*, n.s., 4 vols., Oxford: Clarendon Press, 1952.

Foster, W., ed., *The English Factories in India*, Oxford: Clarendon Press, 1906–27.

Fox, R., ed., *Realm and Region in Traditional India*, New Delhi: Vikas, 1977.

Frykenberg, R.E., ed., *Land Control and Social Structure in Indian History*, Delhi: Oxford University Press, 1979.

Furber, Holden, *John Company at Work: A Study of European Expansion in India in the late Eighteenth Century*, New York: Octagon Press, 1970.

———, *Rival Empires of Trade in the Orient 1600–1800*, Minneapolis: University of Minnesota Press, 1976.

Glamann, K., *Dutch-Asiatic Trade, 1620–1740*, Copenhagen/The Hague: Martinus Nijhoff, 1958.

Habib, Irfan, *Atlas of the Mughal Empire*, Delhi: Oxford University Press, 1982.

Habib, Irfan and T. Raychaudhuri, eds., *The Cambridge Economic History of India*, vol. I, Cambridge: Cambridge University Press, 1982.

Hadaway, W.S., *Cotton Painting and Printing in the Madras Presidency*, Madras: Madras Monographs No. 13, Government Press, 1917.

Hall, K.R., *Trade and Statecraft in the Age of the Colas*, Delhi: Abhinav Publications, 1980.

Hamilton, C.G., *Trade Relations between India and England, 1600–1896*, Calcutta: Thacker, Spink & Co., 1919.

Heras, H., *Studies in the Aravidu Dynasty of Vijayanagar*, Madras: G. Paul & Co., 1927.

Hickey, W., *Tanjore Maratta Principality in South India*, Madras: C. Foster & Co., 1872.

Holder, E., *Monograph on Dyes and Dyeing in the Madras Presidency*, Madras: Madras Record Office, 1896.

Irwin, J. and P.R. Schwartz, *Studies in Indo-European Textile History*, Ahmedabad: Calico Museum of Textiles, 1966.

Karashima, N., *Towards a New Formation: South India under Vijayanagar Rule*, Delhi: Oxford University Press, 1992.

Khan, S.A., *The East India Company Trade in the 17th Century in its Economic and Political Aspects*, London: Oxford University Press, 1923.

Khan, Y.H., ed., *Farmans and Sanads of the Deccan Sultans*, Hyderabad, 1963.

Kling, B.B. and M.N. Pearson, eds., *The Age of Partnership: Europeans in Asia before Dominion*, Honolulu: University of Hawaii Press, 1979.

Leach, E. and S.N. Mukherjee, eds., *Elites in South Asia*, Cambridge: Cambridge University Press, 1970.

Leur, J.C. van, *Indonesian Trade and Society*, The Hague: W. Van Hoeve, 1955.

Lombard, Denys and Jean Aubin, eds., *Asian Merchants and Businessmen in the Indian Ocean and the China Sea*, Delhi: Oxford University Press, 2000.

Love, H.D., ed., *Vestiges of Old Madras*, 3 vols., London: Murray, 1913.

Mahalingam, T.V., *Economic Life in the Vijayanagar Empire*, Madras: University of Madras, 1951.

———, *Administration and Social Life under Vijayanagar*, pt I, Madras: University of Madras, 1969; pt II, Madras: University of Madras, 1975.

Malleson, G.B., *History of the French in India*, London: W.H. Allen, 1893; Cambridge University Press, rpt, 2010.

Moreland, W.H., *From Akbar to Aurangzeb: A Study in Indian Economic History*, London, 1923; Delhi: Munshiram Manoharlal, rpt, 1972.

Mukund, K., *The Trading World of the Tamil Merchant*, Hyderabad: Orient Longman, 1999.

Parthasarathi, P., *The Transition to a Colonial Economy: Weavers, Merchants and Kings in South India, 1720–1800*, Cambridge Studies in Indian History and Society, Cambridge: Cambridge University Press, 2001.

Pavlov, V.I., *Historical Premises for India's Transition to Capitalism*, Moscow, 1978; Delhi: Manak Publications, 2000.

Pearson, M.N., *Merchants and Rulers in Gujarat*, Berkeley: University of Minnesota Press, 1976.

________, *Before Colonialism: Theories on Asian-European Relations, 1500–1750*, Delhi: Oxford University Press, 1988.

Prakash, Om, *The Dutch East India Company and the Economy of Bengal, 1630–1720*, Princeton: Princeton University Press, 1985.

________, *European Commercial Enterprise in Pre-Colonial India*, The New Cambridge History of India, vol. II, pt. 5, Cambridge Paperbacks, 2000.

Rajayyan, K., *Rise and Fall of the Poligars of Tamilnadu*, Madras: University of Madras Press, 1974.

Raju, Sarada, *Economic Conditions in Madras Presidency*, Madras: University of Madras, 1941.

Ramaswamy, Vijaya, *Textiles and Weavers in Medieval South India*, New Delhi: Oxford University Press, 1985.

Rao, V. Narayan, D. Shulman and Sanjay Subrahmanyam, *Symbols of Substance: Court and State in Nayaka Period Tamilnadu*, Delhi: Oxford University Press, 1998.

________, *Textures of Time*, Delhi: Permanent Black, 2001.

Raychaudhuri, Tapan, *Jan Company in Coromandel Coast, 1605–1690: a study in the interrelations of European commerce and traditional economics*, The Hague, 1962.

Richards, D.S., ed., *Islam and the Trade of Asia*, Pennsylvania: University of Pennsylvania Press, 1971.

Richards, J.F., *Mughal Administration in Golconda*, Delhi: Oxford University Press, 1975.

________, *The Mughal Empire*, The New Cambridge History of India, vol. I, pt. 5, South Asian edn, Cambridge University Press, 1998.

________, ed., *Precious Metals in the Later Medieval and Early Modern Worlds*, Durham: Carolina Academic Press, 1981.

Rothermund, D., *Asian Trade and European Expansion in the Age of Mercantilism*, New Delhi: Manohar, 1981.

Sainsbury, E.B., ed., *A Calendar of the Court Minutes, etc. of the East India Company*, Oxford: Clarendon Press, 1935.

Sardesai, G.S., *New History of the Marathas*, 3 vols., Bombay, revd. edn, 1956, vol. I, pp. 215–25.

Sarkar, Jadunath, *History of Aurangzeb*, 5 vols., Calcutta: M.C. Sarkar and Sons, 1912–30.

________, *Fall of the Mughal Empire*, 4 vols., Hyderabad: Orient Longman, rpt, 2007.

Sarkar, J.N., *The Life of Mir Jumla, the General of Aurangzeb*, Calcutta: Thacker, Spink & Co., 1951; 2nd revd. edn, Delhi, 1979.

________, *Studies in Economic Life in Mughal India*, Delhi: Oriental Publishers and Distributors, 1975.

Sastri, K.A.N., *History of South India*, 3rd edn, Madras: Oxford University Press, 1966.

———, *South India and Southeast Asia: Studies in their History and Culture*, Mysore: Geetha Book House, 1978.

Sastry, K.R.R., *South Indian Guilds*, Madras: Indian Publishing House Ltd., 1925.

Seth, Mesrovb Jacob, *The Armenians in India from the Earliest Times to the Present Day: A Work of Original Research*, Calcutta, 1937; New Delhi: Asian Educational Services, rpt, 1992.

Sherwani, H.K., *History of the Qutb Shahi Dynasty*, New Delhi: Munshiram Manoharlal, 1974.

Sherwani, H.K. and P.M. Joshi, eds., *History of Modern Deccan, 1295–1724*, 2 vols., Hyderabad: Government of Andhra Pradesh, 1973.

Srinivasachari, C.S., *History of Gingee and its Rulers*, Annamalai: Annamalai University Press, 1943.

———, *History of the City of Madras*, Madras: P. Varadachary & Co., 1939.

Steensgard, N., *The Asian Trade Revolution of the 17th Century: The East India Companies and the Decline of the Caravan Trade*, Chicago: University of Chicago Press, 1974.

Stein, B., *Essays on South India*, Delhi: Oxford University Press, 1975.

———, *South Indian Temples*, Delhi: Oxford University Press, 1978.

———, *Peasant State and Society in Medieval South India*, Delhi: Oxford University Press, 1980.

———, *All the King's Mana: Papers on Medieval South Indian History*, Madras, 1984.

Stephen, Jeyaseela S., *Portuguese in the Tamil Coast: Historical Explorations in Commerce and Culture 1507–1749*, Pondicherri: Navajothi, 1998.

Subrahmanyam, Sanjay, *The Political Economy of Commerce: Southern India, 1500–1650*, Cambridge: Cambridge University Press, 1989.

———, *Improvising Empire: Portuguese Trade and Settlement in the Bay of Bengal, 1500–1700*, Delhi: Oxford University Press, 1990.

———, *The Portuguese Empire in Asia, 1500–1700: A Political and Economic History*, London and New York: Longman, 1993.

———, ed., *Merchants, Markets and the State in Early Modern India*, Delhi: Oxford University Press, 1990.

Thurston, E., *The Cotton Fabric Industry of the Madras Presidency*, Madras: Madras Government Press, 1897.

———, *Castes and Tribes of Southern India*, 6 vols., Madras, 1909.

Tuck, Patrick, ed., *The East India Company: 1600–1858*, vol. I—W. Foster, *England's Quest of Eastern Trade*, London: Routledge, rpt, 1998.

Vriddhagirisan, V., *The Nayaks of Tanjore*, Annamalai: Annamalai University Press, 1942; New Delhi: Asian Educational Services, rpt, 1995.

Wallerstein, Immanuel, *The Modern World System: Capitalist Agriculture and the Origins of the European World-Economy in the Sixteenth Century*, New York: Academic Press, 1974.

———, *The Modern World System II: Mercantilism and the Consolidation of the European World-Economy, 1600–1750*, New York: Academic Press, 1980.

Wheeler, J.T., *Madras in the Olden Times*, 3 vols., Madras: Graves & Co., 1860–62.

_______, *Early Records of British India*, Calcutta: Thacker, Spink & Co., 1879; New Delhi: Asian Educational Services, rpt, 1972.

Wilson, H.H., *Descriptive Catalogue of the Mackenzie Collections*, Asiatic Press, 1928; *The Mackenzie Collection*, Government Oriental Manuscripts Library, 2009.

Winius, G.D. and M.P.M. Vink, *The Merchant-Warrior Pacified: The VOC (the Dutch East India Company) and its Changing Political Economy in India*, Delhi: Oxford India Paperbacks, 1994.

Articles

Abraham, M.M., 'A Medieval Merchant Guild of South India', *Studies in History*, vol. IV, no. 1, 1982, pp. 1–26.

Alam, Muzaffar and Sanjay Subrahmanyam, 'Exploring the Hinterland: Trade and Politics in the Arcot Nizamat (1700–1732)', in *Politics and Trade in the Indian Ocean World: Essays in Honour of Ashin Das Gupta*, R. Mukherjee and L. Subramanian, eds., Delhi: Oxford University Press, 1998, pp. 113–64.

Arasaratnam, S., 'Some Aspects Relating to the Establishment and Growth of European Settlements along the Tamil Coast in the Seventeenth Century', *Tamil Culture*, vol. 7, 1958, pp. 355–69.

_______, 'The Dutch East India Company and the Kingdom of Madura 1650–1700', *Tamil Culture*, vol. 12, 1963, pp. 48–74.

_______, 'Indian Merchants and their Trading Methods, *c.* 1700', *Indian Economic and Social History Review*, vol. 3, no. 1, 1966, pp. 85–95.

_______, 'Mare Clausum: The Dutch and Regional Trade in the Indian Ocean, 1650–1740', *Journal of Indian History*, vol. LXI, pts 1–3, 1983, pp. 73–91.

Bayly, C. and S. Subrahmanyam, 'Portfolio Capitalists and the Political Economy of Early Modern India', S. Subrahmanyam, ed., *Merchants, Markets and the State in Early Modern India*, Delhi: Oxford University Press, 1990, pp. 242–65.

Brennig, J.J., 'Chief Merchants and the European Enclaves of 17th Century Coromandel', *Modern Asian Studies*, nos. 2–3, 1977, pp. 321–46.

_______, 'Textile Producers and Production in late 17th Century Coromandel', S. Subrahmanyam, ed., *Merchants, Markets and the State in Early Modern India*, Delhi: Oxford University Press, 1990, pp. 66–89.

_______, 'Joint Stock Companies of Coromandel', *The Age of Partnership: Europeans in Asia Before Dominion*, B.B. Kling and M.N. Pearson, eds., Honolulu: University of Hawaii Press, 1979, pp. 71–94.

Calkins, P., 'The Formation of a Regionally Oriented Ruling Group in Bengal, *1700–1740*', *Journal of Asian Studies*, vol. XXIX, no. 4, August 1970, pp. 799–806.

Chaudhuri, K.N., 'The Structure of the Indian Textile Industry in the Seventeenth and Eighteenth Centuries', *Indian Economic and Social History Review*, vol. XI, nos. 2–3, 1974, pp. 127–82.

de Souza, T.R., 'Marine Insurance and Indo-Portuguese Trade History: An Aid to Maritime Historiography', *Indian Economic and Social History Review*, vol. XIV, no. 3, 1977, pp. 377–84.

Dodwell, H., 'The Madras Weaver under the Company', *Proceedings of the Indian Historical Records Commission*, 1922, pp. 41–7.

Glamann, K., 'European Trade, 1500–1750', in *The Fontana Economic History of Europe, Vol. II, the Sixteenth and Seventeenth Centuries*, ed. C.M. Cipolla, London: Collins/Fontana Books, 1974, pp. 427–526.

Habib, Irfan , 'Potentialities of Capitalistic Development in the Economy of Mughal India', *Journal of Economic History*, vol. XXIX, no. 1, 1969, pp. 32–78.

———, 'The Technology and Economy of Mughal India', *Indian Economic and Social History Review*, vol. XVII, no. 1, 1980, pp. 1–34.

Lewandowski, Susan, J., 'Changing Form and Function in the Ceremonial and the Colonial Port City in India: An Historical Analysis of Madurai and Madras', *Modern Asian Studies*, vol. 11, no. 2, 1977, pp. 183–212.

Nield-Basu, Susan, 'The Dubashes of Madras', *Modern Asian Studies*, vol. 18, no. 1, 1987, pp. 1–31.

Perlin, Frank, 'Proto-Industrialization and Pre-Colonial South Asia', *Past and Present*, vol. 98, 1983, pp. 30–95.

Poonen, T.I., 'Early History of the Dutch Factories of Masulipatam and Petapoli', *Journal of Indian History*, vol. 27, no. 3, 1949, pp. 261–94.

———, 'Anglo-Dutch Relations in India Proper (The Earliest Phase, 1602–1627)', in two parts, *Journal of Indian History*, vol. 27, no. 1, 1950, pp. 9–22.

Pearson, M.N., 'Political Participation in Mughal India', *Indian Economic and Social History Review*, vol. IX, no. 2, 1972, pp. 113–31.

Qaisar, A.J., 'Merchant Shipping in India during the Seventeenth Century', *Medieval India: A Miscellany*, vol. II, pp. 195–220.

Ramaswamy, V., 'Some Inquiries into the Condition of Weavers in Medieval South India', *Indian Historical Review*, vol. VI, nos. 1–2, 1970–80, pp. 119–40.

Raychaudhuri, T., 'European Commercial Activity and the Organisation of India's Commerce and Industrial Production', in *Readings in Indian Economic History*, ed. B.N. Ganguly, Bombay: Asia Publishing House, 1964, pp. 64–77.

Richards, J.F., 'European City-States on the Coromandel Coast', in *Studies in the Foreign Relations of India: Prof. H.K. Sherwani Felicitation Volume*, ed P.M. Joshi and M.A. Nayeem, Hyderabad: State Archives, 1975, pp. 508–21.

———, 'The Imperial Crisis in the Deccan', *Journal of Asian Studies*, vol. 35, no. 2, February 1976, pp. 237–56.

Rudner, D.W., 'Religious Gifting and Inland Commerce in 17th Century South India', *Journal of Asian Studies*, vol. 46, no. 2, 1987, pp. 361–79.

Saletore, B.A., 'Some Aspects of the Overseas Trade of Vijayanagar from the Accounts of European Travellers', in *B.C. Law Commemoration Volume*, ed. D.R. Bhandarkar, Calcutta, 1945.

Sarkar, J.N., 'The English at Madras and Mir Jumla', *Journal of Indian History*, 1941.

Sherwani, H.K., 'The Reign of Abdullah Qutb Shah', in two parts, *Journal of Indian History*, 1964.

Srinivasachari, C.S., 'The Madras Council and its Relations with the Golconda Administration under Madanna and Akanna', *Journal of Indian History*, 1931.

Stein, B., 'Coromandel Trade in Medieval India', in *Merchants and Scholars*, ed. J. Parker, Minneapolis, 1965.

_______, 'The State and the Agrarian Order in Medieval South India', *Essays on South India*, New Delhi: Oxford University Press, 1975.

_______, 'Integration of the Agrarian System of South India', in *Land Control and Social Structure in Indian History*, ed. R.E Frykenberg, New Delhi, 1979.

Subrahmanyam, Sanjay, 'The Portuguese, the port of Basrur and the Rice Trade', in *Merchants, Markets and the State in Early Modern India*, Delhi: Oxford University Press, 1990, pp. 18–47.

_______, 'Asian Trade and European Affluence: Coromandel, 1650–1750', *Modern Asian Studies*, vol. 22, no. 1, 1988, pp. 179–88.

_______, 'Persians, Pilgrims and Portuguese: The Travails of Masulipatnam Shipping in the Western Indian Ocean, 1590–1665', *Modern Asian Studies*, vol. 22, no. 3, 1988, pp. 503–30.

Venkatrama Aiyer, K.R., 'Medieval Trade, Craft and Merchant Guilds in South India', *Journal of Indian History*, vol. XXV, pts. 1–3, 1947, pp. 269–80.

Wallerstein, I., 'Incorporation of the Indian Subcontinent into Capitalist World-Economy', in *The Indian Ocean: Explorations in History, Commerce and Politics*, ed. Satish Chandra, Delhi, pp. 222–53.

Index